CW01335619

Stop Overthinking with Ikigai

Transform Negative Spirals and Self-Sabotage into Purpose and Zen Clarity

BERNADETTE SAKURAI

Copyright © 2024 by Bernadette Sakurai

All rights reserved. No part of this publication may be reproduced, stored or transmitted in any form or by any means, electronic, mechanical, photocopying, recording, scanning, or otherwise without written permission from the publisher.

It is illegal to copy this book, post it to a website, or distribute it by any other means without permission.

First edition

Table of Contents

Introduction: A Journey from Overthinking to Inner Purpose..... 7

The Cycle of Overthinking and Self-Doubt................................. 9

Why Japanese Wisdom? 11

Introducing Ikigai: A Path to Purpose and Peace 15

Moving from Overthinking to Meaningful Action 16

What to Expect from This Book 16

Chapter 1: The Reality of Overthinking and Self-Sabotage 19

The Presence of Overthinking in Everyday Life 19

Types of Overthinking and Their Real-Life Examples 20

Chapter 2: Japanese Philosophies as a Solution 29

Why Ancient Japanese Wisdom Resonates with Modern Western Lives 29

A Brief Introduction to Essential Japanese Philosophies 30

Chapter 3: Types of Overthinking and Japanese Philosophies as Solutions... 39

Rumination... 39

Worry About the Future 41

Indecision 42

Perfectionism 44

Catastrophizing 46

Procrastination 48

Self-Sabotage 51

Ikigai: A Holistic Framework for Reducing Overthinking 52

Integrating Ikigai with Balanced Living: Lessons from the Okinawan Lifestyle 53

Chapter 4: The Dual Approaches to Ikigai 58

The Western Model of Ikigai: The Four Circles of Purpose ... 59

The Traditional Japanese Approach: Embracing Simple Joys and Everyday Harmony 68

Comparing and Integrating the Two Approaches to Ikigai 77

Chapter 5. Exercises to Discover Your Ikigai 83

Exploring Passion: What Do You Love? 83

Uncovering Mission: What Does the World Need? 86

Identifying Profession: What Are You Good At? 88

Creating Vocation: What Can You Be Paid For? 90

Finding Harmony: The Balance of Ikigai's Four Elements 92

Integrating the Four Elements: Crafting Your Ikigai Statement 94

Modern Applications of Mindfulness for a Busy Life 106

Integrating Mindfulness and Ikigai: Creating a Mindful Routine 110
Frequently Asked Questions 147
Reflections on My Path 152
References 153

Introduction: A Journey from Overthinking to Inner Purpose

Have you ever felt trapped in an endless loop of thoughts, unable to find peace? Overthinking is more than a habit — it's a thief of clarity and purpose. It has woven itself into our daily lives, often pulling us into negative spirals fueled by the unending pace of modern living and the relentless pressure to succeed. With minds racing from one thought to the next, decision-making feels paralyzing, and the prospect of peace seems just out of reach. This book is for anyone seeking to break free from the cycle of overthinking and rediscover a calm, purposeful way forward.

Yet beyond the tangled web of overthinking lies another nagging feeling—that sense of purposelessness, as if something vital is missing. Have you ever felt like your life is going well enough, yet wondering how you arrived at this stage or where your path is genuinely leading? Sometimes, even though we seem to be doing everything "right," the deep fulfillment we crave remains elusive. Many of us ask, "What happened to the dreams I once had"? "Why do I feel adrift?" If any of this resonates with you, know you are far from alone.

This sense of drifting without purpose, the perpetual nagging feeling that there must be something more, is all too common in today's fast-paced world. Often, it manifests as a mix of overthinking, second-guessing, and self-sabotage. You may find yourself constantly questioning every decision, overanalyzing every possibility, and searching for meaning in things that once felt certain. It's an exhausting cycle; the more you try to think out of it, the more trapped you feel. But there is another way—to reconnect with a deeper sense of purpose and reclaim the peace that overthinking and aimlessness have taken away.

"He who has a why to live can bear almost any how."

— **Friedrich Nietzsche**

In the following chapters, we'll explore how Japanese philosophy—particularly the concept of ikigai—can provide a fresh perspective on breaking free from negative spirals. Unlike the standard Western self-help model, which often emphasizes achievement and measurable success, Japanese wisdom offers a more holistic approach to peace, purpose, and fulfillment. This book isn't just about escaping overthinking; it's about discovering a path toward a purposeful life that resonates with who you truly are.

This book offers insights and practical tools for managing overthinking and embracing purpose. It is important to note that the information and resources provided are meant for personal growth, mindfulness, and managing overthinking. This is not a substitute for professional medical advice, diagnosis, or treatment. If you are experiencing severe stress, anxiety, depression, or other mental health challenges, please seek assistance from a licensed mental health professional or healthcare provider. Remember, reaching out for support is a strength, not a weakness.

First, let's examine what it means to struggle with overthinking and why so many people are affected by it today.

The Cycle of Overthinking and Self-Doubt

When life feels overwhelming, the mind often tries to make sense of it by overanalyzing every detail. Overthinking can seem harmless or even useful at first. Perhaps you replicate conversations, question decisions, or agonize over past mistakes. Gradually, it transforms from reflection into rumination, from planning into paralysis. You may notice that this thinking keeps you stuck rather than propelling you forward.

These negative spirals take many forms, each compounding the sense of being stuck or overwhelmed:

1. **Rumination:** Dwelling on past events, dissecting each interaction and mistake. Rather than learning from these experiences, you find yourself repeatedly drawn to them, searching for answers or hoping that understanding will bring peace.
2. **Constant Worry:** Projecting adverse outcomes into the future. You may think about everything that could go wrong or obsess over how every decision you make today could lead to unintended or even catastrophic consequences tomorrow.
3. **Indecision and Paralysis:** With so many possibilities and paths, the fear of making the "wrong" choice becomes overwhelming. Instead of moving forward, you find yourself stuck, overthinking every option.
4. **Perfectionism and Self-Sabotage:** Striving to get everything precisely correct may seem like a noble goal, but

it often leaves us immobilized, fearing mistakes or avoiding action altogether.

If you've experienced any of these, overthinking has likely woven into your daily life, shaping your decisions, outlook, and self-perception. Each form feeds into negative spirals, creating loops of self-doubt and worry that can feel impossible to escape without deliberate intervention.

Are You Living Someone Else's Dream?

Many people reach adulthood and realize that their lives don't align with who they feel inside. They may have followed paths laid out by societal expectations, family pressures, or career demands. Still, they lost sight of their dreams somewhere along the way. Instead of creating a life driven by passion and purpose, they feel stuck on autopilot.

This disconnection from purpose often manifests as a quiet, but persistent feeling that something is missing. You may be doing well in your career, maintaining good relationships, and meeting society's expectations, but deep down, you wonder if this is your life. Where did my dreams go? How did I get here? And is this the life I want for myself?

It's easy to ignore these questions and keep pushing forward. After all, we're often taught that hard work and success are the keys to happiness. But as you may have discovered, there's a difference between external success and internal fulfillment. Achievements can bring temporary satisfaction, but without a more profound sense of purpose, that satisfaction can quickly fade, leaving you craving more.

Before we dive deeper, I want to share my story—how overthinking consumed my life and how I found these principles to transform.

A Turning Point in My Journey

Like many of you, I've been a "black-belted overthinker". The turning point came during a family trip to Japan when a casual dinner conversation transformed into a life-changing experience. I was talking to a friend about my studies, my work as a coach, my endless overthinking, and the feeling of being stuck, even when things seemed fine on the surface. My friend paused and asked, "I can see how passionate you are about helping others—could this be your ikigai?" I froze. That single question planted a seed in my mind.

I had spent so much time searching for purpose in external achievements, chasing goals, and meeting expectations. Yet, I had never considered that my ikigai might already be within me, waiting to be discovered. That night, I couldn't sleep. I kept replaying the conversation and reflecting on the parts of my life that made me feel alive, connected, and fulfilled. For the first time, I thought I was starting to understand what I was missing. My path forward was clear—I needed to reconnect with the ancient Japanese wisdom that my family heritage hinted at but that I had never fully explored.

Why Japanese Wisdom?

In recent years, Japanese wisdom has gained significant traction in the Western world, becoming a cornerstone of modern self-help and lifestyle trends. Concepts like ikigai (life's purpose), shinrin-yoku (forest bathing), and kintsugi (the art of embracing imperfection by repairing broken items with gold) have sparked interest far beyond their cultural origins. Why do these ideas resonate so profoundly with people today? The answer lies in their holistic, grounded approach to fulfillment—a perspective that feels like a breath of fresh air compared to the high-pressure, goal-oriented mindset that dominates much of Western self-improvement.

The Growing Appeal of Japanese Concepts

The Western world has long been drawn to ideas that promise balance and simplicity, and Japanese philosophies deliver exactly that. Practices like shinrin-yoku encourage us to reconnect with nature, offering a meditative, restorative experience far removed from modern life's digital distractions and urban chaos. Similarly, kintsugi drives us to value imperfections, transforming what we might perceive as flaws into a source of strength and beauty. In a world that often demands perfection and constant achievement, these ideas offer an antidote: they remind us to slow down, accept what is, and find meaning in the everyday.

At the heart of this growing trend is ikigai, a philosophy that integrates purpose, fulfillment, and practicality in a way that feels accessible to people from all walks of life. Unlike many Western self-help approaches that focus solely on reaching ambitious goals or achieving external success, ikigai invites us to find joy in the present moment while aligning our lives with deeper values.

Eastern vs. Western Perspectives on Purpose

Japanese philosophies like ikigai contrast profoundly with Western approaches to purpose and fulfillment. While Western ideals often focus on outward achievements and measurable success, Japanese wisdom invites us to explore balance, harmony, and inner fulfillment. Western self-help emphasizes measurable outcomes, such as career milestones, financial goals, and personal achievements. These pursuits, while motivating, can create a sense of urgency that fosters stress and burnout when progress stalls. In contrast, Japanese philosophies such as ikigai and shouganai prioritize integrating purpose into everyday life, guiding individuals to find peace even in mundane tasks.

Eastern philosophies, particularly those rooted in Japanese culture, shift the focus from grand accomplishments to cultivating inner balance and alignment. Ikigai, for instance, states that purpose lies in the small joys of daily life, emphasizing the journey over a distant destination. While Western ideals may encourage creating a five-year career plan, Japanese approaches like ikigai and shogunai guide individuals to live in the present, finding meaning even in seemingly simple tasks.

Ikigai, for instance, is not a singular, fixed goal but a dynamic balance of what we love, what we're good at, what the world needs, and what we can be paid for. This adaptability allows ikigai to evolve alongside us, offering a sustainable sense of meaning throughout different stages of life.

Moreover, Eastern philosophies like mushin (no mind) and shouganai (acceptance) guide us to let go of rigid expectations and embrace life as it unfolds. They remind us that fulfillment is not about controlling every aspect of our lives but finding harmony in the present moment, even amidst challenges. In an era of constant demands and uncertainty, the Japanese approach reminds us that true fulfillment isn't a race to win but a journey to be savored. We can rediscover the peace and clarity we often seek by welcoming balance, connection, and the present moment. By shifting the focus from strict standards to adaptability and mindfulness, Eastern philosophies offer a sustainable antidote to modern pressures.

Understanding these differences allows us to adopt a balanced perspective, combining Western self-help's focus and ambition with Eastern philosophies' grace and harmony. By blending both, we can work toward our goals with clarity while remaining deeply connected to our personal values.

Why This Perspective Matters Now

As modern life becomes increasingly complex, people search for ways to simplify and reconnect with themselves, their purpose, and the world around them. Japanese wisdom offers a holistic approach that addresses individual well-being and fosters a deeper connection to others and the environment. By implementing practices like ikigai, shinrin-yoku, and kintsugi, we can break free from the cycle of overthinking and rediscover the beauty of living intentionally.

These philosophies show us what to aim for and how to live with more presence, gratitude, and resilience. They offer tools for navigating life's challenges with grace and purpose, providing a roadmap that feels particularly vital in a time when so many feel disconnected or overwhelmed.

Introducing Ikigai: A Path to Purpose and Peace

Ikigai is more than just a concept; it's a way of life that invites us to align our actions, values, and goals with our inner essence. When we have a purpose that makes our heart beat faster, a reason that inspires us to get up each morning, life's path becomes simpler. With a clear purpose, the number of decisions we face diminishes, stress levels drop, and moments of harmony increase.

In the traditional Japanese view, ikigai doesn't necessarily refer to a grand, overarching life purpose. It can be as simple as the joy of a morning walk, the satisfaction of cooking a meal, or the pleasure of caring for a loved one. Ikigai gives us a sense of meaning and fulfillment, no matter how big or small.

In recent years, Western culture has adopted a model of ikigai that involves finding the intersection of four key elements: what you love, what you're good at, what the world needs, and what you can be paid for. While this model explains how ikigai applies to careers and ambitions, it needs to capture the full depth of the Japanese concept. Traditional ikigai embraces the small joys and the larger aspirations, creating a holistic sense of purpose that isn't dependent on external success.

In this book, we'll explore both interpretations of ikigai—the Western model and the traditional Japanese perspective—and show how each can bring clarity and direction to your life.

Discovering ikigai allows you to untangle yourself from overthinking, self-doubt, and purposelessness that may have held you back for too long.

Moving from Overthinking to Meaningful Action

Suppose you've ever been paralyzed by indecision or self-doubt. In that case, you're likely aware of how overthinking can prevent you from living the life you truly want. Overthinking creates mental roadblocks that make it challenging to take action, even when the path forward is clear. In Japanese philosophy, there is an understanding that clarity and purpose come not from analyzing every possible outcome but from taking small, intentional steps forward. When you operate from a place of purpose, the mind naturally quiets down as it focuses on what truly matters.

A key principle in Japanese philosophy is kaizen—continuous improvement. Kaizen emphasizes that growth occurs gradually by making small adjustments in actions, thoughts, and attitudes. It trains us to overcome perfectionism and take small, actionable steps toward ikigai.

What to Expect from This Book

In the coming chapters, we'll examine the root causes of overthinking, indecision, and self-doubt and how these habits contribute to a sense of purposelessness. We'll explore the different types of overthinking—such as rumination, constant worry, indecision, and perfectionism—and how they create barriers to a fulfilling life. For every kind of overthinking, we'll introduce a Japanese philosophy to help counteract these tendencies.

Here's what you can expect:

1. **Understanding the Problem:** We'll start by exploring the nature of overthinking and self-sabotage, examining how these patterns emerge and why they can be difficult to escape.
2. **Japanese Wisdom as a Solution:** Next, we'll introduce various Japanese philosophies—such as ikigai, wabi-sabi, shouganai, and kaizen—and how they can offer unique, practical approaches to finding peace and purpose.
3. **Applying Japanese Wisdom to Overthinking:** In this section, we'll pair each form of overthinking with a relevant Japanese concept, demonstrating how these philosophies provide specific tools for overcoming mental roadblocks.
4. **The Two Approaches to Ikigai:** We'll examine the Western ikigai model of four intersecting circles and the traditional Japanese perspective, showing how each approach can help you clarify your life's purpose.
5. **Practical Steps Toward Ikigai:** Finally, we'll discuss actionable steps to integrate ikigai into your daily life, from mindfulness exercises to cultivating Zen Clarity, a state of calm focus that fosters a deeper connection with your purpose.

A Fresh Direction Ahead

Moreover, this book is about more than finding answers. It's about cultivating a mindset that allows you to approach life with curiosity, openness, and appreciation for each moment. Combining Japanese philosophy's wisdom with practical exercises and reflections gives you a toolkit for transforming overthinking into purposeful living. Ikigai is not a destination but a journey that begins with a single step.

Whether you're here because you feel disconnected from your life, weighed down by stress, frustrated after trying other methods to manage overthinking, or simply curious about a new perspective, this book is for you. Let's embark on this journey together and find the peace, purpose, and fulfillment that may have felt out of reach for so long.

Chapter 1: The Reality of Overthinking and Self-Sabotage

"The mind is its own place, and in itself can make a heaven of hell, a hell of heaven."

— John Milton

The Presence of Overthinking in Everyday Life

Overthinking begins subtly, with a brief worry or doubt. As these thoughts repeat, they echo in our minds, creating self-doubt, hesitation, and purposelessness patterns. If not addressed, overthinking can develop into a mindset that fosters stress, anxiety, and a feeling of being trapped.

Many people struggle with overthinking, and while it might appear harmless or helpful, isn't careful thought a sign of intelligence? — It often leads to self-sabotage, which inhibits us from pursuing goals and finding fulfillment. Let's explore how overthinking manifests daily and creates obstacles to inner peace, clarity, and direction. As we delve into the roots of overthinking, we'll explore how Japanese philosophies offer profound solutions to these patterns, creating a balance between acceptance and action.

Types of Overthinking and Their Real-Life Examples

Overthinking can take various forms, each with a unique impact on our lives. Here, we'll examine some common types of overthinking, illustrated with examples from people like Rachel, Ethan, Claire, Daniel, and Erik. Their stories reflect everyday struggles and make us understand these patterns more personally.

1. Rumination: The Trap of Reliving the Past

Rumination is a cycle of rethinking and replaying past events, like conversations, choices, mistakes, or feedback you get. Instead of offering insight, rumination keeps us fixed in place, rehashing old pain rather than learning from it and moving forward.

Example: Rachel, a project manager, often finds herself stuck replaying recent events, such as a well-received work presentation. Despite positive feedback, she kept revisiting the presentation, imagining every word she could have said better. This obsession makes her anxious and uncertain, diminishing her ability to focus on future projects. Despite her track record of success, her mind is held captive by what she perceives as her "mistakes," filling her with regret and self-doubt.

The toll of rumination is real—it prevents us from moving forward. It blocks us from seeing our worth, undermining self-confidence and creating an inner landscape of worry and regret.

2. Constant Worry: Fixating on the future

The "what-ifs" of life can be overwhelming, filling us with dread about potential scenarios and pitfalls. Constant worry often centers on hypothetical negative outcomes, which keeps us paralyzed in fear rather than engaged in productive action.

Example: Ethan, a talented young graphic designer, feels trapped in his freelancing career. Though his skills are sought after, he constantly worries about finding consistent work and how every project impacts his future stability. His mind swirls with questions like, What if I fail? What if I can't find enough clients? As a result, Ethan hesitates to accept challenging projects, fearing they might end badly or confirm his doubts about his skills.

The grip of future worry keeps Ethan from taking meaningful risks that could grow his career. Instead of allowing him to explore opportunities, his mind constantly seeks to protect him from failure, ironically preventing him from achieving his full potential.

3. Indecision and Paralysis: The Fear of Making the Wrong Choice

Sometimes, the more options we have, the harder it becomes to choose, as the fear of making a mistake can cause indecision and a reluctance to commit. This type of overthinking often leaves us feeling powerless and unable to take action.

Example: Daniel, a successful engineer, feels ready for a change in his career but cannot leap. He evaluates his options repeatedly, considering every "what if" scenario, but fears the consequences of leaving his secure job. Every option seems risky, leading to endless analysis and an inability to act. He remains in the same role, unsatisfied and afraid of the unknown.

Daniel's struggle illustrates how overthinking can lead to "analysis paralysis," in which we're so busy weighing options that we lose the ability to move forward. For Daniel, this pattern keeps him tied to an unfulfilling job, slowly draining his motivation.

4. Perfectionism: Striving for Flawlessness at All Costs

Perfectionism is the need to achieve flawless results, often motivated by fear of criticism or failure. While high standards can drive excellence, the fixation on perfection can paralyze us, creating fear and self-sabotage.

Example: Claire, a teacher and mother of two, feels constant pressure to be the perfect parent and role model. She scrutinizes every decision about her children's education and activities, worrying that one misstep could harm their futures. Her perfectionism keeps her on edge and prevents her from enjoying motherhood. She spends so much time analyzing her decisions that it drains her energy and leads to frequent stress.

For Claire, perfectionism feels necessary, but it actually traps her in an exhausting cycle of worry and self-criticism. Instead of feeling like she's thriving in her roles, she feels inadequate, constantly second-guessing herself. Perfectionism often works against us, fueling anxiety and undermining our sense of accomplishment.

5. Over-Analysis: The Endless Quest for Information

Sometimes, pursuing knowledge and preparation can turn into over-analysis. This habit disguises itself as a caution but prevents progress. Over-analysis often creates a sense of doubt, as there's always more information to consider.

Example: Lucas, a digital nomad and freelance web developer, is endlessly researching the next step in his career. He feels like there's always something he doesn't know or an approach he hasn't fully considered. The result? He keeps putting off decisions, waiting for the "perfect" moment when he feels fully prepared. However, that moment never arrives, leaving him stranded in a cycle of gathering information without action.

Lucas's story demonstrates the pitfalls of over-analysis. Although gathering information is wise, excessive analysis keeps him rooted in uncertainty and unable to move forward. Instead of feeling more confident, he becomes more doubtful and hesitant with every new piece of information.

6. Catastrophizing: Imagining the Worst Possible Outcomes

Catastrophizing is the habit of expecting the worst, imagining worst-case scenarios that fill us with dread and anxiety. This type of overthinking is draining and often makes minor issues seem insurmountable.

Example: Ethan, already prone to worry about his future, often imagines his career crashing down. A client's delayed response convinces him he must have made a terrible mistake. Instead of waiting calmly for clarification, he fills his mind with worst-case scenarios, imagining his reputation ruined. Catastrophizing erodes Ethan's sense of security, making everyday situations seem like potential disasters.

When catastrophizing, minor concerns spiral into significant fears, distorting reality and creating stress. This cycle not only consumes time but also robs us of our sense of peace, turning ordinary problems into sources of paralyzing anxiety.

7. Relationship Overthinking: The Need for Approval

In relationships, overthinking often manifests as needing reassurance, replaying conversations, or analyzing intentions. The fear of miscommunication or conflict can consume our thoughts, leading to self-doubt and anxiety.

Example: Rachel often questions her relationships, especially with her close friends and colleagues. After every interaction, she replays the conversation, wondering if she said something wrong or offended someone. This constant overthinking leaves her feeling uncertain about her connections, and she often seeks validation, asking others if they're "okay" with her.

Rachel's overthinking of relationships strains her friendships and keeps her from feeling secure. Her constant need for reassurance weakens her confidence, preventing her from enjoying genuine connection. She fixates on minor details and misses the joy of authentic relationships.

How Overthinking Leads to Self-Sabotage and a Sense of Aimlessness

Overthinking doesn't just create mental strain; it significantly affects all aspects of life. As we've seen in these examples, different types of overthinking—rumination, future worry, or catastrophizing—lead us to self-sabotage, often unconsciously. Let's examine how overthinking impacts mental and physical health, relationships, and our overall sense of purpose.

Mental and Physical Health

A study by Dr. Susan Nolen-Hoeksema at Yale University investigated the psychological and physical effects of overthinking. The research revealed that individuals prone to rumination are significantly more likely to experience anxiety and depression, as well as a range of physical symptoms like chronic headaches and digestive issues. The study also showed that the mental toll of overthinking can lead to sleep disturbances, which in turn contribute to increased stress and a weakened immune system. [1]

Nolen-Hoeksema's research highlights that rumination doesn't lead to problem-solving, as overthinkers might believe; instead, it contributes to an ongoing loop of distress that has tangible health consequences. This study supports that breaking free from overthinking can improve mental and physical health, underscoring the importance of managing these thought patterns.

For instance, Ethan's constant worry about his career prospects fills him with anxiety, affecting his sleep and leaving him feeling tired and irritable. The toll of overthinking drains him emotionally and makes him less capable of tackling the challenges he fears.

Impact on Relationships

Overthinking affects how we relate to others. It often leads to unnecessary strain in friendships, family relationships, and professional connections. Seeking approval, fearing judgment, and replaying conversations can weaken our connections as people sense our insecurity or notice our need for constant reassurance.

Rachel's tendency to overanalyze her interactions prevents her from being fully present with friends and family. Her need to "fix" imagined mistakes creates tension, making relationships feel more like obligations than sources of support and joy.

Career and Personal Fulfillment

Professionally, overthinking inhibits creativity, reduces productivity, and limits career growth. It can lead to missed opportunities, as the fear of failure prevents us from taking risks. This, in turn, creates a feeling of stagnation as we realize we're not moving forward or developing in meaningful ways.

Daniel's inability to decide on a new career path has kept him stuck in a role he no longer enjoys, sapping his motivation and sense of fulfillment. Instead of feeling purposeful, he feels trapped, aware of the need for change but unable to make it happen.

The Path Forward

Overthinking, self-sabotage, and feeling lost are not isolated problems; they're interconnected patterns that reinforce one another, creating a problematic cycle that is difficult to escape. However, these patterns are not unbreakable. Understanding the roots of overthinking and exploring alternative ways to approach life's challenges can shift our perspective and build a purposeful and fulfilling life.

Overthinking can feel inescapable. However, centuries-old Japanese philosophies offer a way to break free, restoring balance, clarity, and purpose. In the following chapters, we'll explore how Japanese philosophy, emphasizing balance, simplicity, and inner clarity, provides a new approach to these age-old problems. Concepts like ikigai, kaizen, wabi-sabi, and zen clarity offer practical solutions and a deeper understanding of how to create meaning in our lives. Zen Clarity, in particular, counters the mental chaos of overthinking by guiding us toward simplicity and intentional living. In light of this exploration, you'll learn how to replace the need for control with accepting life's natural flow, transforming overthinking into a purposeful pathway.

Staying within the familiar comfort zone can limit our growth, and many pay a high price for it in the form of apathy or even depression. Pushing our boundaries is a natural part of who we are. Still, as we grow older, we become acutely aware of our vulnerabilities and what we stand to lose. So, we often choose to stay within what's known—even if it doesn't truly fulfill us—rather than risk stepping into the unknown. Yet, we can only grow and find a new purpose by accepting the unfamiliar.

In this journey, the goal isn't to eliminate all thoughts but to reframe them, guiding you toward a grounded, purposeful, and uniquely your own life.

Chapter 2: Japanese Philosophies as a Solution

"If you want to find the universe's secrets, think about energy, frequency, and vibration."

— **Nikola Tesla**

The wisdom of Japanese culture provides an antidote to the relentless cycle of overthinking. Philosophies like ikigai and kaizen show us how to navigate challenges intentionally and gracefully.

Why Ancient Japanese Wisdom Resonates with Modern Western Lives

The fast-paced Western world, with its emphasis on productivity, efficiency, and achievement, has led many to experience high levels of stress, anxiety, and a sense of purposelessness. More and more, people are searching for a reprieve from the demands of daily life and ways to regain a sense of inner peace and clarity. As we look for alternatives, many turn to ancient Eastern philosophies—particularly those rooted in Japanese culture—for guidance. These methods, shaped by centuries of experience, emphasize resilience, simplicity, and a balanced approach to life that is often absent in Western ideologies.

Japanese wisdom has gained popularity in Western countries because it doesn't impose rigid structures or strict doctrines.

Instead, it offers gentle, practical concepts that can be adapted to each individual's lifestyle.

Let's explore some of the most influential Japanese philosophies and how they solve the pervasive problem of overthinking in Western lives today.

A Brief Introduction to Essential Japanese Philosophies

Japanese wisdom is a vast field, but certain philosophies have stood out for their relevance and transformative power. These include kaizen, shouganai, mushin, wabi-sabi, and kintsugi. Each of these addresses a unique aspect of overthinking, offering an approach that reduces mental clutter and fosters a deeper connection with the present moment and the self.

1. Kaizen: The Philosophy of Continuous Improvement

The staircase of kaizen shows how small, consistent steps lead to meaningful progress, emphasizing the power of gradual improvement.

Kaizen translates to "change for the better" and is often associated with incremental progress and minor improvements. Initially popularized in the Japanese workplace as a method for enhancing productivity, kaizen has been embraced worldwide as a principle for self-improvement and personal growth.

Kaizen tackles overthinking by breaking down large, daunting goals into manageable steps. When we overthink, we often become overwhelmed by the enormity of our ambitions or the fear of making mistakes. Kaizen counters this by encouraging small, consistent actions that lead to meaningful change. This approach fosters productivity and cultivates mental clarity by breaking the chains of procrastination and hesitation. For example, suppose Rachel, the project manager struggling with perfectionism, applied kaizen. In that case, she might begin by taking five minutes each morning to prioritize her tasks rather than attempting to plan her entire day in one sitting. By focusing on small improvements, she could reduce her stress and accomplish more with less anxiety.

The beauty of kaizen lies in its simplicity. Instead of striving for perfection, it asks us to engage in steady, achievable progress. Over time, these small steps accumulate into significant change, alleviating the pressure to achieve everything at once and supporting us to break free from the cycle of overthinking.

2. Shouganai: The Art of Acceptance

The bending tree embodies shouganai, teaching us to let go of resistance and accept what cannot be changed, finding strength in adaptability.

Shouganai can be translated as "it cannot be helped" or "it is what it is." This philosophy emphasizes accepting circumstances we cannot change and adapting to life's unpredictability. Rather than wasting energy resisting what we cannot control, shouganai encourages us to flow with life's challenges.

In the context of overthinking, shouganai is incredibly powerful. Many types of overthinking—such as constant worry, rumination, and catastrophizing—stem from an inability to accept uncertainty. For Ethan, the freelance graphic designer worried about his career stability; shouganai could remind him that certain aspects of his professional life, like client demands or economic fluctuations, are beyond his control. Instead of obsessing over hypothetical outcomes, he could focus on what he can influence, freeing his mind from unnecessary stress.

Shouganai educates that surrendering to life's inevitable ups and downs doesn't mean giving up; instead, it allows us to direct our energy toward what truly matters. This acceptance reduces the mental strain caused by overthinking, replacing anxiety with a sense of calm and resilience.

3. Mushin: The State of "No Mind"

The Zen Enso circle symbolizes Mushin, or 'no-mind,' where clarity and focus arise by staying fully present and free from distraction.

Mushin, meaning "no mind," refers to a mental state free from distractions and unnecessary thoughts. Often practiced in martial arts and meditation, mushin is the ability to focus entirely on the present moment without interference from fears, doubts, or past experiences. It aligns the mind with the task at hand, making it highly relevant for those struggling with perfectionism and indecision.

For Claire, the perfectionist teacher and mother, mushin could be transformative. Her constant need to achieve flawless results leads her to overthink even the most minor decisions, robbing her of peace. By practicing mushin, she could train herself to focus on what she's doing in the present, free from the weight of future anxieties or past mistakes. This approach allows her to be fully engaged and effective in each task without the interference of perfectionism or self-criticism.

The essence of mushin is presence. When we engage fully with each moment, overthinking fades, and we become more productive, creative, and at peace. By letting go of the "clutter" in our minds, we can find clarity and purpose in our actions.

4. Wabi-Sabi: Embracing Imperfection

This delicate branch of cherry blossoms represents finding beauty in impermanence, simplicity, and life's fleeting moments. Each petal reminds us to embrace imperfections and cherish the present.

Wabi-Sabi is the philosophy of finding beauty in imperfection and embracing the transient nature of life. Rooted in the Japanese appreciation for simplicity and natural beauty, wabi-sabi drives us to value authenticity over perfection and find joy in life's "imperfect" parts.

Wabi-Sabi directly counters overthinking by challenging the pursuit of perfection that often fuels self-doubt and anxiety. For Daniel, an experienced engineer stuck in his career, wabi-sabi could be a powerful antidote to his fear of change. Rather than waiting for the "perfect" opportunity or the "perfect" decision, he could embrace the idea that life's beauty lies in its unpredictability and impermanence. This acceptance can reduce the pressure to make flawless choices, allowing him to move forward with a lighter heart.

Wabi-Sabi encourages us to appreciate the journey, imperfections, and all. By accepting life's inherent messiness, we can alleviate the stress and pressure that often lead to overthinking. Instead of striving for a flawless life, we learn to value what we have, releasing ourselves from the endless pursuit of "more" and focusing instead on what brings us genuine joy.

5. Kintsugi: The Art of Repairing with Gold

This kintsugi bowl shows that imperfection and impermanence can reveal unique beauty and value.

Kintsugi, or "golden joinery," is the Japanese art of repairing broken pottery with lacquer mixed with powdered gold. Rather than hiding the cracks, kintsugi highlights them, creating a unique, beautiful piece that celebrates its history and imperfections. This philosophy embodies resilience, turning damage into beauty and strength.

For Lucas, the digital nomad plagued by overanalysis, kintsugi offers a powerful metaphor. Instead of fixating on every decision to avoid "mistakes," he could approach each choice as an opportunity for growth. If a choice leads to unexpected outcomes, kintsugi expresses that these "cracks" aren't failures but chances to learn and grow. This shift in mindset transforms fear of failure into a celebration of resilience and adaptability.

Kintsugi assists us in reframing mistakes and setbacks, viewing them as valuable aspects of our personal journey. By celebrating our imperfections and "cracks," we gain freedom from overthinking and become more open to life's possibilities. Each experience, even those marked by challenges, becomes a golden thread woven into the fabric of our unique story.

Ikigai: A Holistic Solution for Inner Harmony and Purpose

This compass represents ikigai, guiding you toward a fulfilling and balanced life by aligning your passions, skills, and the world's needs.

Ikigai stands out among Japanese philosophies because it encompasses a holistic approach to life's meaning and purpose. Often translated as "reason for being," ikigai invites us to examine the intersection of four key elements: what we love, what we are good at, what the world needs, and what we can be paid for. These areas of life come together to form our ikigai, the driving purpose that brings fulfillment and joy.

However, ikigai is more than a career tool or a way to pursue grand ambitions. Traditional Japanese culture views ikigai as both profound and simple—the satisfaction of a day's work, the joy of a small accomplishment, the warmth of a cherished hobby. It's a balance and harmony that encompasses life's little pleasures and larger aspirations.

For those burdened by overthinking, ikigai offers a meaningful path forward. Each of the previously discussed philosophies—kaizen, shouganai, mushin, wabi-sabi, and kintsugi—supports the pursuit of ikigai by assisting us embrace simplicity, resilience, and clarity. Integrating these elements allows us to break free from mental clutter and build a life centered on what truly matters.

"Your Ikigai is at the intersection of what you are good at and what you love, but it's also about what you believe the world needs."

— **Hector Garcia**, Ikigai: The Japanese Secret to a Long and Happy Life

By discovering our ikigai, we can cultivate a life that feels meaningful, balanced, and uniquely ours. By focusing on actions and pursuits that resonate with our core values, we can alleviate overthinking and live with greater purpose and peace. When we have a clear purpose, the number of decisions we face naturally decreases, and we don't need to fear that solutions will be lost if our minds aren't constantly racing. When we're caught up in endless mental chatter, we don't find answers—we only create new problems. Shifting into a mindful, 'no-mind' state allows space for images, ideas, and solutions to emerge naturally. Things often fall into place independently when we're on the right path. Let's not be afraid to follow our instincts because our ikigai will not lead us astray.

As we explore these philosophies further, we'll see how they address the most common types of overthinking—offering practical methods to reclaim clarity and purpose.

Chapter 3: Types of Overthinking and Japanese Philosophies as Solutions

"Fall seven times, stand up eight."

— **Japanese Proverb**

Each form of overthinking presents unique challenges. However, Japanese philosophies like wabi-sabi and mushin provide targeted tools to overcome them.

Rumination

Rumination, or the tendency to dwell on past mistakes or regrets, is a typical pattern in overthinking. When we repeatedly revisit old conversations or actions, we trap ourselves in a loop that keeps us from moving forward. The philosophies of kintsugi and wabi-sabi are especially useful in addressing rumination by encouraging us to embrace imperfections and view past experiences as valuable parts of our journey.

Implementing Kintsugi: Finding Beauty in the Broken

Kintsugi, the art of repairing broken pottery with gold, demonstrates that our "cracks" make us unique. Here are some ways to apply kintsugi principles to reduce rumination:

Reflection Journaling: Write down specific moments from the past that you frequently ruminate on. Reflect on how these experiences have contributed to who you are today, even if painful. Describe the "golden lines" these experiences left in your life, turning your focus from regret to gratitude.

Forgiveness Practice: Kintsugi also speaks to the power of forgiveness—of self and others. Practicing forgiveness can help close the loop of rumination. Each day, spend a few minutes forgiving yourself for past mistakes. Remind yourself that each "break" has added value to your life.

Practicing Wabi-Sabi: Embracing Life's Imperfections

Wabi-Sabi invites us to see beauty in the imperfect and impermanent. Applying this mindset can break the cycle of rumination by transforming our perspective on the past.

Find meaning in the Unfinished: Reflect on projects or relationships that ended before you felt they were "complete." Consider that their imperfection is part of their beauty. By shifting your focus to the value of each experience, regardless of its "finish," you can begin to release the past.

Meditate on Nature: Wabi-Sabi often draws inspiration from nature's cycles. Spend time observing nature, watching leaves fall or a flower's growth. Nature's imperfections remind us that beauty lies in the cycle of life, encouraging us to let go of rigid expectations.

"Accepting your flaws is not weakness; it's wisdom."

— **Japanese Proverb**

Worry About the Future

Constant worry about future uncertainties can lead to stress and paralyzing fear. The Japanese concepts of shouganai (acceptance of what cannot be controlled) and shinrin-yoku (forest bathing) can center us in the present moment, reducing the burden of future-oriented anxieties.

Practicing Shouganai: Letting Go of What You Can Not Control

The shouganai principle encourages acceptance of events beyond our control. It's not about resignation but about freeing ourselves from the constant mental strain of trying to control the uncontrollable.

Identify the Unchangeable: List things you're currently worrying about. Divide this list into "within my control" and "beyond my control" columns. Let yourself let go of the items in the second column, focusing only on what you can influence.

Daily Acceptance Affirmations: Begin each day with an affirmation of acceptance, such as "I accept what I cannot change and trust that I can handle whatever comes." This daily practice of acceptance can gradually shift your mindset and lessen future-oriented worries.

Engaging in Shinrin-Yoku: Grounding Yourself in Nature

Shinrin-Yoku, or forest bathing, refers to spending time immersed in natural settings to improve well-being. Research shows that nature exposure reduces stress hormones and eases anxieties about the future.

Mindful Walks in Nature: Set aside 10-15 minutes for a daily walk in a nearby park, focusing on the sensory experience of your surroundings. Pay attention to the sounds, scents, and colors of nature. As your mind becomes absorbed in the present, worries about the future naturally fade.

Grounding Techniques with Nature: If you're indoors, keep elements of nature nearby—a small plant, stones, or essential oils. Whenever future worries arise, touch these objects and take a few deep breaths, reminding yourself to return to the present.

"In every walk with nature, one receives far more than he seeks."

— **John Muir**

Indecision

Indecision often stems from overanalyzing options, which can feel overwhelming. The Japanese concepts of kaizen (continuous improvement by small steps) and shuhari (a martial arts principle for gradual mastery) provide frameworks for overcoming indecision by emphasizing incremental progress and experiential learning.

Applying Kaizen: Taking Small, Manageable Steps

Kaizen advocates breaking down tasks into small, achievable steps. For those struggling with indecision, this method reduces the pressure to make "perfect" choices and encourages action by simple steps. By focusing on steady improvement, kaizen allows us to let go of overwhelming expectations, reduce the negative spirals of doubt and worry, and foster a sense of mental clarity.

The One-Minute Rule: Start by taking just one minute of focused action on a decision you're struggling with. Whether you're researching options, drafting an email, or writing out pros and cons, beginning breaks the inertia of indecision.

Daily Progress Check-ins: At the end of each day, list one small step you took toward a decision. Over time, these small steps build momentum, reducing the tendency to overthink every option.

Focus on Progress, Not Perfection: Decisions don't have to be perfect; they just need to move you forward. Trust that even small actions will guide you toward clarity.

Practicing Shuhari: Learning Through Stages

Shuhari is a framework for mastering new skills in stages: Shu (learn and follow the basics), Ha (break away and explore variations), and Ri (transcend and create your own). It conveys that mastery requires patience and that gradual exploration can overcome indecision.

Adopt a Beginner's Mindset: Approach new choices as a beginner, allowing yourself to make imperfect decisions without judgment. Remember that each option is a learning opportunity rather than a test of expertise.

Stage-Based Progression: Break decisions into three stages. First, gather basic information (Shu), then explore options more freely (Ha), and finally, make a choice based on your insights (Ri). This method encourages growth and reduces the pressure of making the "perfect" decision.

"A journey of a thousand miles begins with a single step."

— Lao Tzu

Perfectionism

Perfectionism, driven by fear of mistakes or judgment, can create constant stress and immobilize us. Wabi-Sabi, with its appreciation for imperfection, and mushin, the state of "no mind," both encourage us to take action without the need for perfection, freeing us from the constraints of overthinking.

Adopting Wabi-Sabi: Finding Value in Imperfection

Wabi-Sabi reminds us that beauty often lies in the imperfect. For perfectionists, adopting this philosophy means learning to value authenticity over flawlessness.

Imperfect Action Practice: Each week, choose a task to complete imperfectly, whether a quick drawing, a handwritten note, or an informal email. Gradually, you'll become comfortable with imperfections and see that authenticity is often more meaningful than "perfect" results.

Create "Imperfect" Art: Engage in a creative activity that naturally embraces flaws, like painting, pottery, or crafting. As you work, focus on the uniqueness of each stroke or mark rather than aiming for a flawless product. This practice shifts your perspective on perfectionism in other areas of life.

Practicing Mushin: Acting Without Overthinking

Mushin, or "no mind," is a state of focused, effortless action. For those trapped by perfectionism, mushin encourages doing rather than overthinking.

Focus on Flow: Set a timer for 15-20 minutes and engage in a task without stopping to review or correct. During this time, let go of your inner critic, allowing yourself to experience the flow of the task itself. Practicing flow gradually transfers your attention from the results to the process.

Breath-Based Centering: Practice mindful breathing for one minute before beginning a task. To do this, sit comfortably, close your eyes, and take a slow, deep breath through your nose for a count of four. Hold your breath for a count of four, then exhale slowly through your mouth for a count of four. Repeat this cycle. Each time you feel the urge to overthink or self-criticize, return to your breath. This focus on the present moment cultivates the "no mind" state, quieting the perfectionist tendencies.

"When you do something, you should burn yourself completely, like a good bonfire, leaving no trace of yourself."

— **Shunryu Suzuki**

Catastrophizing

Catastrophizing, or envisioning the worst-case scenario, can make even minor challenges feel like crises. This overthinking is exhausting and often leads to inaction, as fear overshadows reality. The Japanese philosophies of shouganai (accepting what cannot be changed) and mushin (state of "no mind") both offer ways to release these fear-based thoughts and replace worry with constructive action.

Practicing Shouganai: Accepting the Unpredictable

Shouganai unveils that some events and outcomes are beyond our control. By internalizing this philosophy, we can stop catastrophizing by learning to accept that life's challenges are not always avoidable but manageable.

The "Let Go" Journal: Each time you imagine the worst-case scenario, write down the situation and list the things you cannot control. Next, acknowledge the unpredictable elements and practice releasing your hold on them. Over time, this exercise builds a habit of acceptance and reduces catastrophizing tendencies.

Daily "Release" Ritual: Reflect on the day's worries for five minutes before bed. Visualize them in your hands, then imagine setting them down or releasing them into the air. This mental exercise in letting go can be a helpful way to end the day on a note of peace, diminishing the pull of catastrophizing.

Reframe the Narrative: Shift your focus by asking, "What is the most likely outcome?" This question redirects the mind from unrealistic fears to a balanced perspective, reducing emotional overwhelm.

Applying Mushin: Embracing Action over Worry

Mushin encourages a mind free from needless thoughts and judgments. For those prone to catastrophizing, mushin promotes action over worry, allowing you to engage fully in the present without the distraction of imagined fears.

Mindful Breath: Each time you feel your mind drifting toward a worst-case scenario, take a moment to focus on your breath. Deep, rhythmic breathing can ground you, centering your awareness in the present. This practice redirects mental energy from catastrophic thoughts to what's happening here and now.

Immediate Action Step: When faced with a stressful situation, immediately take a small, constructive action rather than analyzing all possible outcomes. For instance, if you worry about a project deadline, work on one small section instead of dwelling on the consequences of failure. Practicing immediate action reorients focus from imagined fears to practical steps, helping you cultivate a state of mushin.

"Today is the tomorrow we worried about yesterday."

— **Dale Carnegie**

Procrastination

Procrastination is a universal challenge, often fueled by the inner dialogue of doubts, perfectionism, or avoidance. Rather than purely a time management issue, procrastination frequently stems from underlying psychological barriers: fear of imperfection, decision paralysis, or unpreparedness. The immediate relief from stress and anxiety that may accompany inaction is often illusory and fleeting. Be aware of the dangers of inaction because it may lead to a perpetual cycle of avoidance, ultimately undermining one's potential for success and fulfillment. Here's where Japanese philosophies offer a new perspective, addressing both procrastination's emotional and practical aspects.

Practical Ways to Implement Kaizen to Overcome Procrastination:

Kaizen, the principle of continuous improvement, breaks down large tasks into manageable steps, which can significantly reduce the mental load associated with starting a new project. This philosophy encourages us to focus on taking just one small action, making the task seem less daunting and allowing us to make steady progress without overthinking.

Start small: Choose the simplest possible first step related to the task. If writing a report, open a new document and type the title. If organizing files, set aside one folder to sort. Set a goal of two minutes only. Starting small reduces resistance and proves that beginning isn't as difficult as anticipated. Momentum starters often lead to further progress once the first hurdle is overcome.

Progress Visualization: Use a visual tracker—like a calendar, checklist, or progress bar—and update it each time you complete a small action toward the larger task. For example, add a sticker or mark a checkbox each time you complete a 15-minute work segment. Seeing visible progress motivates and reinforces that each effort contributes to the end goal, making the journey rewarding and reducing the urge to delay.

"Procrastination is one of the most common and deadliest of diseases, and its toll on success and happiness is heavy."

— **Wayne Gretzky**

Kaizen reduces procrastination by removing the psychological barriers that make tasks seem overwhelming by focusing on small, achievable actions.

Practical Ways to Practice Mushin in Daily Tasks:

Mushin translates to "no mind" and is about focusing entirely on a task without judgment, doubt, or mental distractions. For procrastinators, mushin encourages a state of mind where the goal is not perfection but being fully engaged.

Single-Task Focus: Choose one task to work on without interruptions. Silence notifications, clear your workspace, and dedicate a specific time to focus solely on this task. This immersion promotes flow and reduces the urge to shift attention or avoid complex parts.

Mindful Check-Ins: Whenever you feel resistance or the temptation to procrastinate, pause and take a few deep breaths. Centering your mind reduces avoidance tendencies and creates mental space to engage fully.

Incorporating mushin into tasks makes the process itself feel rewarding, reducing the urge to delay and increasing satisfaction.

Practical Applications of Shouganai to Address Procrastination:

Procrastination often involves worrying about outcomes, fearing failure, or dreading complex tasks. Shouganai, the concept of "it cannot be helped" makes us accept aspects of a task we can't control and focus only on what we can influence. This shift in focus can reduce the burden of expectations and alleviate fears that fuel procrastination.

Acceptance Affirmations: Before starting a task, remember that perfection isn't the goal and that some factors (like others' opinions or unforeseeable changes) are beyond your control. Repeat affirmations like, "I accept what I cannot change, and I am free to focus on what I can do."

Fear Journaling: If fear or doubt prevents you from starting a task, write down specific worries, then identify which parts are controllable and which aren't. By recognizing and releasing what you can't control, you can approach the task with greater peace and less fear.

Shouganai reframes procrastination as a manageable response to uncertainty, allowing us to release unproductive worries and act on what truly matters.

Self-Sabotage

Self-sabotage often stems from fear of failure, self-doubt, or worry about imperfections. Japanese philosophies provide valuable insights into overcoming these barriers by encouraging self-compassion, acceptance, and presence. Integrating wabi-sabi, shouganai, and mushin into a resilience-building practice helps to counteract self-sabotaging behaviors.

Practical Steps for Resilience Against Self-Sabotage

Use Wabi-Sabi for Self-Acceptance: Acknowledge that striving for imperfection is a natural part of life. Instead of fixating on flaws or failures, view them as essential growth elements. This mindset can support you escape from self-sabotaging thoughts arising from perfectionism.

Apply Shouganai for Stress Relief: Accept that some things cannot be controlled. When facing situations that trigger self-doubt, remind yourself that some factors are outside your influence and that you are not solely responsible for every outcome.

Adopt Mushin for Mental Freedom: Engage in physical activity, like yoga or a creative hobby, where you can enter a "no-mind" state and let go of self-critical thoughts. This frees you from the fear of judgment and aids you in exploring new avenues without self-imposed limitations.

Example: Claire uses these philosophies to overcome self-doubt in her teaching career. Applying wabi-sabi, she learns to appreciate her unique instructing style, recognizing that imperfections don't detract from her impact. Practicing shouganai, she lets go of concerns over factors she can't control, such as students' situations. Finally, she found joy in spontaneous, creative lessons and noticed her stress levels decreasing. Her newfound mindset also improved her relationship with her children, as she focused on connection rather than control.

Ikigai: A Holistic Framework for Reducing Overthinking

Building Your Ikigai for Everyday Life

Ikigai isn't just a goal; it's a lifestyle that can be woven into each daily action. By aligning daily choices with a sense of purpose, you can alleviate stress, reduce mental clutter, and create a steady foundation for peace.

Reflect on Personal Values: List the things you love and are passionate about. Focus on how each aligns with your career, relationships, and hobbies. This reflection lets you see where your current activities contribute to a meaningful life, naturally reducing overthinking.

Set Purpose-Driven Intentions: Each morning, set an intention based on ikigai, such as "Today, I will help others with my work" or "I will bring creativity into my day." Purpose-driven intentions support staying focused and motivated, guiding your thoughts and actions toward meaningful goals rather than endless contemplation.

Regular Ikigai Check-ins: Review the four pillars of ikigai in your life once a week. Ask yourself if you're engaging in activities that reflect what you love, are skilled at, benefit the world, and provide stability. Adjustments can be made gradually, aligning you with your purpose and reducing the urge to overthink daily decisions.

By integrating these philosophies into your life, each thought pattern—rumination, future worry, indecision, perfectionism, and catastrophizing—can transform into constructive habits. Embracing ikigai as a guiding framework brings each philosophy into harmony, allowing you to live a focused, purposeful, and resilient life.

Integrating Ikigai with Balanced Living: Lessons from the Okinawan Lifestyle

While ikigai—a sense of purpose—plays a pivotal role in a fulfilling and long life, the Okinawan lifestyle reveals that purpose alone isn't enough. To truly thrive, an ikigai-centered life benefits from healthy habits and balanced routines that support physical and mental well-being. Okinawans, known for their extraordinary longevity and resilience, have cultivated a lifestyle centered on community, balanced nutrition, physical activity, and emotional stability, naturally supporting and reinforcing their sense of ikigai. Here are some practical elements inspired by the Okinawan way of life that can enrich physical health and emotional stability.

1. Mindful Eating and the Hara Hachi Bu Rule

One of the most striking aspects of the Okinawan lifestyle is their mindful approach to food. Okinawans practice hara hachi bu, which means "eat until you're 80% full." This concept encourages moderation and prevents overeating, allowing the body to avoid the strain of constant digestion and promoting longevity. Their diet is also high in nutrient-dense, low-calorie foods, including vegetables, seaweed, tofu, sweet potatoes, and fish, which reduce inflammation and increase vitality.

To incorporate hara hachi bu into everyday life, you can try pausing mid-meal to assess your fullness and stopping once you feel comfortably satisfied. This habit promotes physical health and a mindful approach to nourishment. When you practice hara hachi bu, you cultivate self-control and awareness of your body's needs, which extends beyond food and into other aspects of life, including mental and emotional well-being.

2. Physical Activity Integrated into Daily Life

Okinawans stay active throughout their lives, not necessarily doing strenuous exercise but integrating movement into daily routines. Activities like gardening, walking, and household chores are valued forms of exercise. This approach to physical activity keeps them agile, reduces stress, and contributes to their longevity.

Modern life often restricts physical activity to gym sessions, which can feel more like a chore than a pleasure. Instead, take inspiration from Okinawan practices by finding enjoyable ways to stay active that align with your lifestyle and ikigai. Whether taking a walk, practicing yoga, or simply gardening, choosing activities that bring you joy enhances the experience and ensures that movement becomes a sustainable, pleasurable part of your routine.

3. Prioritizing Restful Sleep

Quality sleep is another pillar of the Okinawan lifestyle, vital for mental and physical rejuvenation. While modern cultures often glorify long working hours, Okinawans understand that rest is essential for longevity. Adequate sleep is linked to better cognitive function, lower stress levels, and improved resilience, all of which support an individual's ability to engage with their ikigai.

To enhance sleep quality, consider adopting a consistent bedtime, creating a calming evening routine, and minimizing screen time before bed. These small habits can significantly improve sleep quality, leading to better mood regulation and overall well-being, supporting mental clarity and resilience.

4. Balancing Work and Rest

The Okinawan concept of balance extends to work and rest. They recognize that after periods of hard work, rest is essential to restore energy and maintain health. This approach helps prevent burnout and allows for sustainable productivity. This concept aligns with ikigai by ensuring that our purpose does not become a source of stress but a source of balanced fulfillment.

To apply this principle, incorporate regular breaks into your workday, schedule rest periods after intensive tasks, and take time off when needed. Remember that a fulfilling life includes productive and restorative moments to recharge and reconnect.

5. Building Resilience Through Community

Community bonds are essential in Okinawan culture, where people live in close-knit, supportive communities called moai. These social groups offer emotional support, shared responsibilities, and companionship, fostering resilience against life's challenges. Studies consistently show that strong social connections contribute to lower stress levels, greater resilience, and longer lifespans. [2]

Living with a sense of ikigai benefits from community support, as shared purpose and mutual care reinforce emotional stability and resilience. Building a community around shared interests and values can greatly enhance one's mental well-being, whether with friends, family, or organized groups. Consider nurturing relationships that align with one's ikigai and contribute positively to one's sense of belonging and purpose.

Resilience Through Balance and Purpose

By combining ikigai with these Okinawan lifestyle elements, we cultivate resilience—our ability to cope with and adapt to life's challenges. Resilience is strengthened by finding purpose and supporting it with physical health, community, and a mindful approach to life's rhythms. When we feel that our lives have meaning, we are more motivated to overcome adversity and maintain our mental balance.

The practices inspired by Okinawan life offer a holistic approach to resilience. As you integrate these elements into your life, remember that resilience is not about avoiding challenges but creating a strong foundation that allows you to face them. Combining the wisdom of ikigai with these practices can foster a fulfilling, balanced, and resilient life.

While each philosophy mentioned addresses specific patterns of overthinking, ikigai stands as the guiding compass, harmonizing our passions, purpose, and actions to create a fulfilling life.

Chapter 4: The Dual Approaches to Ikigai

"The meaning of life is to find your gift. The purpose of life is to give it away."

— **Pablo Picasso**

Embracing Ikigai: A Journey to Purpose

If you've made it this far, take a moment to acknowledge yourself. By engaging in these pages, you're already on a transformative journey toward self-discovery, purpose, and deeper fulfillment. This step alone is significant, and just by continuing to read, you've demonstrated the courage and curiosity it takes to explore your life's meaning. This is the foundation of ikigai, an ancient Japanese philosophy that has captivated people worldwide by offering purpose, joy, and motivation to make life feel worth living.

To truly move beyond overthinking, we must align our actions with our deeper purpose. Ikigai offers a dual approach, blending practical frameworks with the beauty of everyday joys.

With ikigai, you're not simply setting goals; you're uncovering a profound sense of purpose that resonates on a deep, personal level. Having a purpose that comes from within—an intrinsic goal driven not by external rewards or expectations but by personal meaning—can be profoundly motivating. Intrinsic goals hold value in themselves, fueling long-term passion and commitment. When we pursue something for our reasons, the journey becomes rewarding in its own right, and achieving the goal brings a profound sense of fulfillment. It's the motivation that transcends obstacles, the focus that keeps you centered, and the joy that turns every small step into something valuable. Let's explore how ikigai can be understood in two ways: the structured Western approach of finding a life purpose at the intersection of passion and skill and the traditional Japanese perspective, which sees ikigai as embracing life's simple joys and quiet harmony. By the end, you'll have the tools to integrate ikigai into your own life. This journey can reduce overthinking, enhance inner peace, and inspire a renewed enthusiasm for each day.

The Western Model of Ikigai: The Four Circles of Purpose

The Western ikigai model is typically represented by a Venn diagram of four overlapping circles that reveal an individual's core purpose at their intersection. Each circle represents a different area of life that contributes to our sense of fulfillment, and these areas overlap where ikigai—our unique, motivating purpose—comes into focus. The circles include:

Passion: What you love

Mission: What the world needs

Profession: What you are good at

Vocation: What you can be paid for

Each area taps into different aspects of self-awareness and external purpose, offering a balanced framework that aligns personal values, strengths, societal contributions, and practical needs. Let's delve into each circle in greater depth, examining how they relate to one another and how they can guide us toward living a meaningful, fulfilled life.

1. Passion: What You Love

The passion circle invites us to explore what we love, including our interests, natural curiosities, and activities that genuinely bring us joy. This circle focuses on intrinsic motivations—those things that make us feel alive and inspired, regardless of external rewards.

Discovering What You Love

For many, finding one's passion involves introspection. Passion isn't just about fleeting hobbies or surface-level interests but about activities that resonate deeply. Ask yourself: What captivates your attention and makes you lose track of time? What types of activities do you find yourself naturally drawn to?

Often, what we love reveals itself in childhood experiences or recurring interests. Reflecting on these can be a starting point for understanding one's passion. Some people find their passions involve creative expression, like art or writing. In contrast, others are drawn to problem-solving, teaching, or outdoor adventures.

Embracing Passion with Purpose

Living with passion doesn't mean we must make every interest a career, but incorporating elements of what we love into daily life enhances our well-being. Whether dedicating time each week to a hobby, finding ways to bring creativity into work, or engaging in activities that allow us to be curious, passion brings vitality to life.

Examples of Passion in Practice

Imagine someone who loves storytelling. Their passion could manifest as a career in writing or journalism or be fulfilled by hobbies like blogging or creating short films. Storytelling is intrinsically rewarding for this person—it's something they would pursue even without monetary reward, simply because it brings joy and fulfillment. Recognizing and incorporating this passion into life can create lasting satisfaction and balance.

"Passion is energy. Feel the power that comes from focusing on what excites you."

— **Oprah Winfrey**

2. Mission: What the World Needs

The mission circle focuses on contributing to society and responding to the needs of others. This aspect of ikigai is about service, connection, and making a difference. In other words, mission aligns with the desire to contribute to something greater than oneself.

Identifying the World's Needs

To understand what the world needs, looking at social, environmental, and economic issues that resonate with us is helpful. This could mean addressing global challenges like climate change, education, or healthcare, or it might involve supporting local community needs, such as mentoring youth or aiding in food distribution initiatives. Mission-based fulfillment often comes from recognizing how to impact those around us, locally or globally positively.

Why Mission Matters

Research consistently shows that contributing to society, even in small ways, boosts personal fulfillment. A study published in The Journal of Positive Psychology found that people who engage in prosocial behavior, like volunteering or mentoring, report higher life satisfaction and a greater sense of purpose. Aligning with a mission we care about offers an anchor in life—a reason to get up each day and engage with the world meaningfully.

Living Your Mission

Mission doesn't always mean working for a non-profit or becoming an activist. Instead, it's about weaving a sense of service into our lives, perhaps by pursuing a career that aligns with societal needs or volunteering regularly. For instance, someone passionate about sustainability might find their mission to promote eco-friendly practices, whether by educating others, supporting green organizations, or simply implementing sustainable habits.

"The best way to find yourself is to lose yourself in the service of others."

— **Mahatma Gandhi**

3. Profession: What You Are Good At

The profession circle focuses on our skills, talents, and areas of expertise. This component of ikigai represents the activities in which we excel, often due to training, experience, or natural ability. Understanding what we're good at guides us to make contributions that feel satisfying and build confidence.

Assessing Your Skills and Strengths

Identifying professional strengths involves both introspection and external feedback. We can ask ourselves: What tasks or challenges do I consistently excel at? Where do others seek my expertise? Reflecting on accomplishments or soliciting feedback from colleagues or mentors can provide clarity.

Natural talents and acquired skills both contribute to this circle. Some people have a natural aptitude for organizing, while others may have developed strong analytical skills during their careers.

Assessing strengths and abilities via personality assessments or skill inventories can make us better understand our professional aptitudes.

Building and Leveraging Skills

While some talents come naturally, others can be developed. For example, someone interested in public speaking may start with anxiety but, with practice, becomes a skilled communicator. Investing in developing strengths enhances our ikigai by allowing us to contribute our best abilities to the world. Kaizen, the Japanese philosophy of continuous improvement, aligns well with this part of ikigai, encouraging us to view our professional lives as an ongoing journey of growth.

Aligning Profession with Passion and Mission

Profession is the "doing" aspect of ikigai—it is where we actively engage our abilities in meaningful ways. When we find that our skills and talents support what we love and what the world needs, we gain a sense of satisfaction. For example, a talented teacher who loves working with children and believes in the value of education is likely to feel fulfilled because their profession, passion, and mission align.

"Choose a job you love, and you will never have to work a day in your life."

— **Confucius**

4. Vocation: What You Can Be Paid For

The vocation circle addresses the practical side of ikigai—earning an income and sustaining oneself financially. While pursuing passions and serving others is fulfilling, we must balance these pursuits with the practical requirement of earning a livelihood. Vocation ensures our purpose is sustainable in the long term.

Finding Balance Between Fulfillment and Financial Security

Vocation isn't simply about making money but about making a living that aligns with one's values and skills. This doesn't necessarily mean turning every passion into a career; instead, it's about understanding which activities can be financially sustaining while offering satisfaction.

The concept of ikigai encourages us to look at vocation as more than a job. It's a way of earning a living that respects personal values and talents. For instance, artists may find financial security by teaching art classes or selling their work, balancing creativity with income.

Creating Multiple Income Streams

Many people today balance multiple sources of income, such as freelance work, side projects, or passive income, allowing them to pursue their ikigai while meeting financial needs. For example, a writer passionate about environmental issues might work as a freelance journalist while creating content for eco-conscious brands on the side. Diversifying income streams is one way to ensure financial security without compromising on passion or mission.

The Role of Vocation in Modern Life

Modern careers no longer follow a linear path; many are multi-passionate and pursue varied interests. This adaptability allows us to shape careers that serve personal fulfillment and financial needs. Finding this balance is often an ongoing process, evolving as we change and the world shifts.

"Work to become, not to acquire."

— **Elbert Hubbard**

Integrating the Four Circles: Finding Your Ikigai

Balancing the elements of ikigai brings not just alignment but also Zen Clarity—a state where decisions and actions reflect harmony with one's true nature.

The beauty of the Western Ikigai model is in how these circles interact. When passion, mission, profession, and vocation overlap, the result is a sense of wholeness. This intersection doesn't just represent a job or a hobby but a deeper alignment where purpose, skill, and practicality converge, offering a life path that is fulfilling on multiple levels.

The Power of Alignment

When we live at the center of these circles, each action and choice feel intentional and impactful. For instance, a doctor passionate about children's health, skilled in medicine, committed to addressing healthcare inequalities and well-compensated for their work embodies ikigai because they are engaged in something meaningful, needed, and financially sustainable.

Moving Toward Your Ikigai

Achieving a perfect balance may take time and adjustments. Some people initially focus on aligning two or three circles, knowing that the complete overlap may evolve as they gain more experience and self-awareness. For example, someone might begin by developing their profession and vocation for personal and professional satisfaction; they may later explore aligning with their passion and mission via volunteering or part-time projects.

Embracing the Process

Finding ikigai isn't about arriving at a destination; it's an ongoing journey. Each choice, experience, and reflection bring us closer to our purpose. For those pursuing ikigai, even small shifts in daily routines, a conscious alignment with personal values, or integrating passions can profoundly impact fulfillment. Whether by self-discovery, service, or career growth, pursuing ikigai is about connecting with a deeper meaning in life, where each moment reflects an authentic sense of purpose. It's worth reflecting on how your current situation affects you. If it negatively impacts your ikigai, it may be time to let it go—no matter how much time or energy you've invested. There's little value in following a path that isn't aligned with what you truly believe in.

The Traditional Japanese Approach: Embracing Simple Joys and Everyday Harmony

The traditional Japanese concept of ikigai does not necessarily refer to a lofty, overarching life purpose or career goal. Instead, it's a more subtle philosophy that enlightens to recognize meaning and joy in daily life's small, often-overlooked elements. Unlike the Western model, which is structured around productivity and goals, the traditional view of ikigai finds meaning in the present moment, and it encourages individuals to nurture simple, consistent practices that enhance both personal well-being and community harmony.

Understanding the Traditional Concept of Ikigai

In Japan, ikigai is often seen as a way of being rather than something to be achieved. It's not about finding a "calling" or a single career path that encompasses all of one's passions and skills; instead, it is an evolving sense of purpose that finds expression in daily rituals, routines, and relationships. For example, a Japanese farmer might find ikigai in planting seeds, nurturing crops, and seeing the rhythm of the life cycle of the seasons. Similarly, a retiree might discover ikigai in caring for grandchildren, cooking traditional meals, or tending a garden. These are not grand ambitions but reflections of deep-seated values that align with life's natural rhythms and the individual's sense of place in the world.

"Ikigai is not something grand or extraordinary. It can be found in the joy of making a perfect cup of tea or the satisfaction of completing a task with care."

— **Ken Mogi,** Awakening Your Ikigai

In this approach, ikigai becomes a guiding philosophy that brings harmony and purpose to life, emphasizing five key principles: Start Small, Release Yourself, Seek Harmony, Find Joy in Little Things, and Live in the present.

Start Small: The Power of Incremental Joy

The Japanese concept of "starting small" aligns closely with focusing on gradual progress rather than immediate achievement. This mindset encourages individuals to focus on one thing at a time, finding contentment and fulfillment in even the smallest of actions. In a world often obsessed with rapid success and large-scale goals, starting small trains us that true growth and satisfaction are found in the present, one small step at a time.

Practicing Small Acts with Purpose

Starting small can mean creating a daily ritual that brings peace or joy, even as simple as preparing tea, arranging flowers, or reading a few pages of a book. These small acts ground us, reminding us of the pleasure of simplicity. By committing to small, meaningful actions each day, we gradually build a life filled with intentional moments that contribute to happiness and purpose.

Example: The Practice of Kaizen in Daily Life

The Japanese principle of kaizen (continuous improvement) also aligns with the Start Small approach, emphasizing that making small, steady improvements to routines or personal habits fosters progress. As these small, intentional changes accumulate, they enhance productivity and create space for mental clarity, helping individuals break free from the negative spirals of doubt and worry. In daily life, kaizen could involve dedicating five minutes daily to a task you've been avoiding or gradually improving a small skill, such as learning a few new words in a foreign language. These incremental steps keep us engaged without overwhelming us, leading to sustainable progress that nurtures personal well-being and fulfillment. Mindfulness and kaizen are deeply connected. Both focus on presence and progress. While mindfulness centers the mind at the moment, kaizen ensures that even small actions move toward meaningful goals. Together, they create a synergy that reduces mental clutter and reinforces a focused, purposeful mindset.

Release Yourself: Letting Go of Ego and Control

In the traditional approach to ikigai, releasing oneself is about letting go of ego-driven desires and the need for control, especially over external outcomes. This principle emphasizes that life is not about chasing status or achieving a "perfect" existence but about learning to accept oneself as part of a larger, interconnected world.

Embracing Humility and Connection

Releasing oneself allows one to focus on the intrinsic value of actions rather than their outcomes. In Japanese culture, humility is deeply valued, and there is a recognition that true fulfillment often comes when we place the needs of others above our own. This could mean practicing kindness, contributing to community well-being, or simply taking pride in one's daily work without seeking accolades.

Practicing Acceptance and Self-Compassion

Self-compassion is a key component of releasing oneself. By releasing the need to be perfect, we can act without fear of failure, enabling us to engage fully in whatever we do. Whether cooking, writing, or engaging in conversation, this acceptance empowers us to avoid overthinking and self-doubt, which can be major roadblocks to peace and joy. Practicing forgiveness of our flaws and missteps encourages a more harmonious relationship with ourselves and others.

"The greatest burden we bear in life is not from others, but from the expectations we place on ourselves."

— **Japanese Proverb**

Seek Harmony: Nurturing Relationships and Connection

In Japanese culture, harmony is a core value, and ikigai often involves contributing positively to family, community, and society. This focus on harmonious relationships emphasizes that our actions should fulfill personal needs and respect and support those around us. We create a network of connections that sustain us by fostering empathy, kindness, and understanding.

Cultivating Wa: The Value of Group Harmony

The concept of Wa, or group harmony, is a central tenet in Japanese society. It encourages individuals to prioritize group well-being over personal ambitions. This is often evident in Japanese workplaces and communities, where collective success and group cohesion are valued as much as if not more than, individual achievement. We can bring this principle into our lives by emphasizing collaboration, listening actively, and making efforts to resolve conflicts amicably.

Finding Balance in Daily Interactions

Seeking harmony means engaging with others thoughtfully and respectfully. Simple acts like practicing patience, actively listening, and showing appreciation can transform relationships and create an environment of mutual support. Harmony in relationships brings a sense of stability and security, grounding us and guiding us to navigate life's challenges with a support system rooted in mutual respect.

Find Joy in Little Things: Embracing Small Moments of Happiness

The traditional approach to ikigai emphasizes finding joy in the little things, a mindset that promotes mindfulness and appreciation for life's simpler pleasures. In Japanese culture, this appreciation is often called mono no aware, a sensitivity to the fleeting beauty of moments and experiences.

The Art of Savoring

Finding joy in the little things means taking the time to savor small, everyday moments that might otherwise go unnoticed. This could be the warmth of sunlight in the morning, the taste of a well-prepared meal, or a brief moment of laughter with a friend. By consciously recognizing these small joys, we train our minds to focus on what is immediately beautiful and gratifying, reducing stress and grounding us in the present.

Practicing Kanso: Simplicity and Minimalism

Kanso, or simplicity, is another Japanese principle that encourages finding beauty in the minimal. Practicing kanso can involve decluttering physical and mental spaces, creating a simpler life where each item, thought, or interaction is intentional. By clearing away unnecessary distractions, we make room for mindful appreciation of the simple joys around us, making engaging with life's inherent beauty easier.

"The world is full of beautiful things just waiting to be noticed."

— **Japanese Proverb**

Live in the Present: Focusing on Now

The final principle of the traditional ikigai approach is to live in the present. Focusing on the present moment is a powerful way to cultivate peace in a world where the mind constantly wanders to future worries or past regrets. This mindfulness practice advices us to fully engage with each experience, bringing clarity and meaning to the simplest tasks and creating space to reflect, prioritize, and act with clarity. From the perspective of ikigai, mindfulness is not just about reducing mental noise—it's about connecting with your deeper purpose.

Mindful Presence in Daily Activities

Living in the present often involves bringing mindfulness into daily routines.

- **Mindful Daily Tasks:** Incorporating mindfulness into everyday activities can make routine tasks meaningful. Whether brewing tea, washing dishes, or walking to work, focus fully on the sensations, movements, and environment around you. These moments of mindfulness are small but powerful steps toward calming an overactive mind.
- **Guided Meditations:** If you struggle with traditional meditation, guided sessions can help focus your thoughts. Apps and online resources provide accessible options, from calming breathing exercises to body scans to reduce stress.
- **Mindful Creativity:** Engage in creative pursuits that demand full attention, such as writing, learning calligraphy, painting, or coloring. Engaging with patterns and designs allows you to stay present, free from judgment or overthinking. My book, *Mindfulness Quotes and Coloring Patterns for Mothers,* offers carefully curated art nouveau patterns and quotes, inviting calm moments and creativity. These activities channel your energy into something productive, leaving little room for overthinking.
- **Mindful Nature Walks:** Practicing shinrin-yoku (forest bathing) is a profoundly mindful way to reconnect with the natural world. Spend time outdoors, paying attention to your surroundings' sounds, smells, and textures. Nature has

a grounding effect, reminding us of our connection to the larger world.

Practicing mindfulness creates heightened awareness and satisfaction. Zen Clarity is the calm focus that emerges when we fully embrace the present moment.

Overcoming Distractions and Practicing Mushin

Incorporating mushin, or a "no-mind" state, can be a powerful tool for living in the present. Like kaizen's principle of breaking tasks into manageable steps, mushin focuses the mind entirely on the task at hand, reducing the overwhelm caused by overthinking. This mental state, free of judgment and distraction, allows us to engage with each moment without interference from self-doubt or anxiety.

Practicing mushin might involve focusing intensely on gardening, cooking, or writing without allowing thoughts to drift elsewhere. Beyond these everyday activities, explore yoga, try a new sport, engage in artistic pursuits, or practice guided meditation. These experiences demand your full attention, leaving little room for overthinking and supporting you in entering a state of mindful presence. Zen clarity emerges when distractions are removed, allowing your mind to settle into a focused, peaceful state. This harmony, fostered using mindfulness and mushin, cultivates a life where each moment feels intentional. It's a reminder that life's most excellent satisfaction often arises from being fully immersed in what we're doing right now.

"When walking, walk. When eating, eat."

— **Zen Proverb**

The Impact of Embracing Everyday Harmony on Life Satisfaction

Studies suggest that living in alignment with these principles enhances well-being and satisfaction. Research from the National Center for Biotechnology Information [3] indicates that focusing on present-moment awareness and engaging in activities that foster personal growth and connection correlates strongly with increased life satisfaction and decreased stress levels. Moreover, a 2020 study on ikigai among older adults [4] found that those who practiced a traditional approach, embracing small, meaningful actions and social harmony, reported higher levels of purpose and lower levels of depression.

In the traditional Japanese view, living with ikigai emphasizes the intrinsic value of life's simple, intentional moments. This philosophy doesn't chase the notion of "finding purpose" in a single job or grand achievement but instead sees purpose as an ever-present opportunity within daily actions, relationships, and personal rituals. By incorporating these five principles—starting small, releasing control, seeking harmony, savoring little joys, and living in the present—ikigai becomes a guide to a balanced, satisfying life. It's a practice of grounded fulfillment, reminding us that true happiness is often found not in what we achieve but in how we live each moment.

Comparing and Integrating the Two Approaches to Ikigai

To fully embrace ikigai, it's crucial to understand how the Western and Japanese perspectives complement each other. They offer a balanced path to fulfillment that addresses our external ambitions and inner peace. Each model addresses different needs and perspectives but can be integrated to bring coherence and balance to our lives. By combining these approaches, individuals can find purpose without sacrificing the joys of everyday living, allowing them to pursue goals with a sense of grounded peace and resilience.

Integrating Purpose with Presence: A Balanced Framework

The Western ikigai model provides a structured approach that is particularly useful for those seeking clarity in their career and life direction. This model focuses on intersecting elements—passion, mission, profession, and vocation—and is inherently goal-oriented. It appeals to those driven by a desire to make a tangible impact on the world, find success, and align their work with their values.

However, while this structure gives clear direction and purpose, it can also lead to stress if interpreted as a constant pursuit of achievement. The Japanese approach to ikigai, which centers on presence, simple joy, and inner harmony, offers a necessary counterbalance. This view encourages individuals to find fulfillment in daily rituals and relationships, recognizing that purpose resides not solely in high-stakes ambitions but in the present moment.

By integrating these two approaches, individuals can simultaneously work towards long-term goals while finding peace in the here and now. For instance, an individual pursuing a career aligned with their mission might focus on their larger goals (as the Western model suggests) but embrace a Japanese approach to ikigai daily by savoring small victories and recharging. This balance helps prevent burnout, enabling sustained growth without sacrificing personal well-being.

Addressing Overthinking and Burnout with Both Approaches

Overthinking and burnout are increasingly prevalent issues in modern life, particularly in Western societies, where productivity and achievement are highly valued. The Western model of ikigai offers direction and helps alleviate overthinking by providing a structured approach to career and personal goals. By categorizing life into passion, mission, profession, and vocation, it allows individuals to focus on one area at a time rather than feeling overwhelmed by a lack of purpose. This structured guidance can significantly reduce rumination, as it provides concrete steps toward fulfillment.

However, while the Western model reduces overthinking in goal-setting, its focus on productivity can lead to burnout. Here, the traditional Japanese perspective of ikigai serves as a powerful antidote. Emphasizing simple joys, mindfulness, and balance, the Japanese model provides practices that counterbalance the stresses of constant achievement. The principle of finding joy in small, intentional acts—like preparing a meal, spending time with family, or enjoying nature—reminds us that fulfillment doesn't have to come only from grand accomplishments.

By combining these models, we gain the benefits of structure and ambition from the Western approach while using the Japanese approach to keep us grounded and prevent burnout. For example, entrepreneurs might set ambitious business goals and use the Western ikigai model to navigate their careers. However, by integrating the Japanese approach, they might also build daily rituals that allow them to recharge, like a morning meditation or evening walk. This balance between focused ambition and restful presence can reduce mental strain, preventing burnout.

"The journey to find purpose need not be a sprint; it can be a steady walk where each moment offers value."

— **Japanese Proverb**

Bridging External Achievement and Inner Fulfillment

One of the unique strengths of the Western ikigai model is its focus on aligning personal strengths and passions with what the world needs. This approach addresses the desire for external impact, offering a structured way to use one's skills to make a meaningful difference. However, it can sometimes overshadow the importance of intrinsic joy and internal fulfillment, as it emphasizes productivity and contribution.

On the other hand, the Japanese ikigai model encourages individuals to find fulfillment in their everyday lives, independent of societal expectations or external achievements. This approach highlights the value of small pleasures and the beauty of imperfection, promoting inner peace. Integrating this perspective with the Western model creates a path that values external contributions and personal success while making room for internal contentment.

For instance, a medical professional might use the Western approach to ensure their career aligns with their skills and the societal need for healthcare, finding satisfaction in their profession. At the same time, they can embrace the Japanese model by focusing on the simple joys of helping each patient and finding meaning in each interaction rather than solely focusing on career milestones. This combined approach ensures that purpose is not exclusively tied to external validation but also deeply rooted in the individual's daily experiences.

Adapting Ikigai to Different Life Stages

The dual perspectives of ikigai also offer flexibility, as different stages of life often demand different approaches to fulfillment. By adapting ikigai to one's life phase, individuals can enjoy a more dynamic, resilient sense of purpose.

Early Career: For those in the early stages of their career, the Western model provides a useful framework for identifying a career path that aligns with their skills, passions, and societal contributions. However, early-career individuals often face intense pressure to succeed quickly, leading to stress. Integrating the Japanese perspective of finding joy in small, meaningful acts can assist them in cultivating patience and resilience, grounding them as they navigate the pressures of career building.

Mid-Career Realignment: Many individuals seek a deeper purpose in mid-career, often moving away from purely career-focused ambitions and toward work-life balance. The Japanese ikigai model can be precious, encouraging them to slow down and enjoy life's simpler pleasures while aligning with their goals. The Western model can guide them in evaluating which professional pursuits still align with their passions and values, making adjustments that bring both external success and inner peace.

Later Life and Retirement: In the later stages, fulfillment often shifts from professional success to personal satisfaction and community connection. The Japanese approach to ikigai aligns well here, as it encourages focusing on relationships, simple joys, and a sense of peace. The Western model still plays a role, as retirees can reflect on ways to use their skills to contribute to their communities. Volunteering, mentoring, or creative pursuits become avenues for purpose, combining both personal fulfillment and societal contribution.

Finding Purpose in Everyday Life: A Practical Synthesis

For ikigai to hold true significance, it must be embodied in long-term pursuits and daily life. The Western model provides a roadmap for achieving larger goals. At the same time, the Japanese approach offers practices that ground us in the present and foster contentment. Integrating these models allows us to structure our lives around intentional progress and the beauty of everyday experiences.

However, the Japanese model adds a layer of adaptability by promoting acceptance and presence. The lesson learned is that obstacles are not just setbacks but opportunities to learn and grow. By integrating both, individuals can maintain resilience while remaining flexible. For example, an entrepreneur facing business setbacks might use the Western approach to reevaluate their strategy while embracing the Japanese philosophy to find peace with current challenges and enjoy small successes.

This synthesis helps individuals approach challenges with a balanced mindset—grounded enough to withstand adversity yet flexible enough to adapt.

My Struggles and Small Wins

Overthinking has been a part of my life for as long as I can remember. I analyze every decision to the point of paralysis, replay conversations in my head, and imagine countless what-if scenarios. My mind was constantly running on overdrive, and I didn't know how to turn it off.

When I began exploring mindfulness as part of my ikigai journey, it was like trying to stop a speeding train with my bare hands. I would sit down, ready to focus on my breath or observe my thoughts, only to find myself spiraling into a mental to-do list or rehashing an old argument. It was frustrating—I felt like I was failing at something basic. But then, something unexpected happened. During one session, I noticed a brief moment of stillness. It wasn't much, but it felt like a victory. From there, I saw other small shifts: the clarity to decide without second-guessing and the ability to let go of a minor mistake. Though they felt insignificant then, these tiny wins were the stepping stones that carried me forward. They showed me that change doesn't have to be immediate or perfect—it just has to begin.

Chapter 5. Exercises to Discover Your Ikigai

The four central elements of ikigai—what you love, what you're good at, what the world needs, and what you can be paid for—serve as a foundational guide to finding your unique purpose. These elements can reveal hidden strengths, passions, or values that can help form a fulfilling life direction. Here, we'll explore self-reflective questions tailored to each area, followed by examples and exercises to bring clarity and focus to your pursuit of ikigai.

Exploring Passion: What Do You Love?

The first component of the Venn diagram, passion, asks us to identify the things we love doing. Passion often emerges in activities that make us lose track of time, that we would pursue even without external rewards, and that fill us with joy and energy. By exploring what you genuinely love, you start uncovering interests that can be cultivated into something more significant. Each discovery contributes to achieving Zen Clarity, a harmonious state where passions align with purpose.

Reflective Questions on Passion

What types of activities make you feel truly alive and engaged? Write uncensored what comes to your mind.

How would you spend your days if money were not an issue?

What topics or skills could you discuss or explore endlessly without getting bored?

When do you experience "flow"—when time seems to disappear because you're so absorbed? Think about things you used to like to dive into that are relevant.

Is there something you've always wanted to try but haven't because you're afraid of failure?

Practical Exercise: The "Passion Discovery List"

To tap into your passions, list 10 activities that bring you joy. For each one, reflect on the following:

Why do I enjoy this activity?

What unique emotions does it bring out?

What personal values or interests does it align with?

For instance, Rachel, a project manager, finds deep satisfaction in mentoring younger team members. Although her job primarily involves managing projects, she realizes that guiding others taps into her love for teaching and helping others grow. By identifying her passion for mentoring, Rachel can look for opportunities to engage in this activity inside and outside her work setting, potentially developing it into a more central part of her ikigai.

"Passion Exploration" Practice

Choose one activity from your list and commit to engaging over the next week. As you do, observe how you feel during and after. Is there a sense of fulfillment? Does it feel like something you'd like to explore more deeply? This practice clarifies the passions you may want to integrate into your life and career.

Uncovering Mission: What Does the World Need?

The "mission" component of ikigai encourages us to look beyond personal satisfaction and consider how we can contribute meaningfully to the world. This can be via community work, addressing social or environmental issues, or simply adding value in areas that positively impact others. Mission-driven purpose gives depth to ikigai by connecting personal strengths with societal needs.

Reflective Questions on Mission

What causes or issues do you feel strongly about?

Are there specific communities, groups, or individuals you want to support or impact?

What problems in the world or your community would you like to help solve?

What role do you want to play in improving the lives of others?

Practical Exercise: The "Value Map"

To connect with your mission, create a "value map." Start by listing issues or groups you care about on a large piece of paper, drawing connections between them, and noting any ideas for contributing. For instance:

Claire, the teacher, realizes she is passionate about educational equity. She wants to help children from underprivileged backgrounds to access quality learning resources. Claire maps out her values around education and social equality, identifying that her job allows her to contribute meaningfully to this mission. As part of her mission-driven ikigai, she starts a community tutoring program for students needing additional support.

"Mission Contribution" Practice

Choose one cause or issue from your value map and brainstorm small, immediate actions you can take to make an impact. For example, you could volunteer, offer mentorship, or donate time to an organization in this area. By taking tangible steps, you align yourself with a purpose beyond personal gain, bringing mission-based activities into your daily life.

Identifying Profession: What Are You Good At?

The 'profession' element of ikigai focuses on your skills and talents—the things you're naturally good at, have worked to develop, or aspire to learn and master in the future. By honing in on these strengths, you can discover areas where you can make significant contributions in your career or other aspects of life. Identifying your profession is especially useful in aligning passion with ability.

Reflective Questions on Profession

What skills do you excel at, even without extensive effort?

In what areas do others often seek your advice, guidance, or assistance?

What feedback have you consistently received about your strengths in both personal and professional settings?

Are there skills or talents you've developed over time that you feel incredibly proud of or excited about mastering in the future?

Practical Exercise: The "Strength Inventory"

Create a "strength inventory" by listing out all of your skills, including those you might overlook as minor. For each skill, write down examples of times you used it successfully and how it benefited others or yourself. Then, rank your skills based on how natural and enjoyable they feel.

For example, as a freelance graphic designer, Ethan lists his creativity, client communication, and problem-solving strengths. He realizes that client communication is something he excels at and enjoys as well, as he finds satisfaction in helping clients clarify their vision. Recognizing this as a core strength, he starts focusing on creative work that involves collaborative client projects, aligning his profession with his natural strengths.

"Skill Expansion" Practice

Select one of your top strengths and dedicate weekly time to improving it. Whether by taking a course, reading, or practicing, this exercise enhances your sense of professional purpose. As you expand this skill, observe how it adds value to your work and relationships, deepening your professional contribution to ikigai.

Creating Vocation: What Can You Be Paid For?

The "vocation" component grounds ikigai in practical reality, focusing on ways to earn a livelihood. By identifying areas where you can apply your skills, passions, or mission in exchange for income, you create a sustainable foundation for purpose. While not every passion or mission translates into paid work, exploring ways to integrate vocation into your life can help make ikigai attainable and realistic.

Reflective Questions on Vocation

Do you offer skills or services that people would pay for?

Have you noticed a demand for a particular talent, product, or service that aligns with your interests?

What financial goals do you have, and how can they intersect with your passion or mission?

Are there alternative ways to earn income through your strengths and interests, such as freelance work, consulting, or side projects?

Practical Exercise: The "Opportunity Brainstorm"

To explore potential vocations:

1. Create a list of ways you could monetize your skills or passions.
2. For each idea, evaluate whether it aligns with your personal goals and values.
3. Consider possibilities beyond traditional employment, such as freelancing, consulting, or creative endeavors.
4. When exploring potential vocations, don't let the thought of others having more expertise or experience hold you back. Your enthusiasm and genuine motivation often matter most; these qualities can make up for gaps in knowledge or skill.

Example: Lucas, the digital nomad, lists various ways to monetize his web design skills. He identifies freelance consulting as a flexible, scalable option that allows him to work remotely while delivering value to clients. Lucas realizes that this vocation supports his lifestyle goals and gives him room to explore other interests, contributing to his ikigai without compromising on financial security.

"Vocation Experimentation" Practice

Select one vocation idea from your list and start testing it in small ways. For instance, take on a freelance project, offer a workshop, or start a side business. By experimenting with potential income sources, you gain firsthand insights into what resonates with your skills and interests while aligning with your financial needs.

Finding Harmony: The Balance of Ikigai's Four Elements

Once you've listed the four elements—what you love, what you're good at, what the world needs, and what you can be paid for—take a moment to look at where they intersect. This intersection is significant because it's where true balance lies. Focusing too much on just one element can lead to an unsustainable life. For example, pursuing your passion without considering financial viability may lead to obsession or burnout, and you may struggle to make a living. Similarly, focusing solely on what you can be paid for may increase your wealth, but still, you may feel spiritually empty and unfulfilled. If what you excel at doesn't align with the community values, you might face isolation and a loss of self-esteem. It's an ongoing task to balance all four elements, ensuring that no single aspect dominates at the expense of the others.

It's also important to recognize that not every activity we love will fit neatly into all four categories, and that's okay. You may have things on your 'what you love' list that don't meet societal needs, require special skills, or offer financial rewards. For example, taking regular walks in the park might not directly impact your career or skill set. Still, it's a supportive ikigai—an activity that refreshes you, sparks creativity, and contributes to your overall well-being. It's essential to nurture these supportive activities as they add richness and depth to your life, reminding us that not everything needs to be monetized or justified by external validation.

Reflection Questions:

Are there any patterns or recurring themes that appear across multiple circles? For example, is there an activity or value that connects what you love, what you're good at, or what the world needs?

If the central overlap feels empty, consider whether negative spirals of doubt or overthinking might hold you back from seeing your true potential. Could it be a skill you still need to develop, a passion you've overlooked, or a need you need to address?

Reflect on your current perception of your abilities. Is there a strength or talent you're undervaluing or taking for granted?

If nothing seems to fit the center right now, what small steps could you take to explore and expand your possibilities? For example, could you try a new hobby, develop a skill, or seek feedback from others about what you excel at?

Imagine your ikigai as a growing seed. What actions or intentions could you plant today to nurture it and allow it to take root in your life?

Integrating the Four Elements: Crafting Your Ikigai Statement

With insights from the exercises above, the next step is to integrate your reflections into a cohesive ikigai statement. This statement serves as a guiding purpose, describing how you want to engage in life that aligns with your values, strengths, and vision. To craft your ikigai statement, combine the elements of passion, mission, profession, and vocation.

Example Ikigai Statements

Rachel's Ikigai Statement: "To inspire and guide others by mentoring, using my leadership skills and love for teaching to foster growth and development in my team."

Claire's Ikigai Statement: "To support educational equity by helping children from underprivileged backgrounds succeed, using my teaching experience to create opportunities for learning and growth."

Lucas's Ikigai Statement: "To use my design skills to help businesses thrive online while maintaining a flexible, location-independent lifestyle that allows for travel and creative freedom."

These statements reflect a personalized, integrated approach that balances passion, mission, profession, and vocation. These ikigai statements can be adjusted and refined over time as individuals grow and explore new paths, allowing for a dynamic, evolving sense of purpose.

By answering these reflective questions and exercises, you gain clarity on what you love, what you're good at, how you can contribute to the world, and how to integrate these into a vocation. This journey towards ikigai is deeply personal and rewarding, leading to a balanced life that respects inner joy and outward contribution.

Practicing Mindfulness and Presence: Exercises for Discovering Small Joys, Finding Harmony, and Living in the Present

Mindfulness practices, like the sensory mapping method and zazen meditation, are not just tools for calming the mind but essential for fostering emotional stability. By grounding ourselves in the present moment, we reduce the mental chaos caused by overthinking and create a balanced state of mind. This stability enables us to approach challenges and decisions with clarity, free from the overwhelm of negative spirals. Mindfulness practices like zazen meditation not only ground you in the present but also significantly reduce anxiety by calming the mind and slowing racing thoughts.

Grounding Yourself with Every Step

Mindful walking is a simple practice that combines physical movement with mental stillness. Here's how:

1. Choose a Quiet Path: Find a space to walk without distractions.

2. Focus on Sensations: Pay attention to the feeling of your feet touching the ground, the rhythm of your breath, and the sights or sounds around you.

3. Anchor in Gratitude: With each step, reflect on one thing you're grateful for. This practice helps you stay present and calm.

At its core, mindfulness involves focusing on the present moment with openness, curiosity, and non-judgment. Practicing mindfulness exercises enables us to let go of distractions and fully engage with our surroundings, actions, and interactions. These practices are precious in pursuing ikigai, allowing us to slow down, appreciate simple joys, and cultivate inner peace.

Here are specific exercises tailored to each aspect of ikigai mindfulness—appreciating small pleasures, finding harmony, and living in the present—with examples and variations that fit modern lifestyles.

1. Discovering Small Joys: Techniques for Heightening Appreciation

Small joys are moments that might otherwise go unnoticed—enjoying a hot cup of tea, watching the sunset, or feeling a gentle breeze. By cultivating awareness of these moments, we can transform ordinary experiences into sources of peace and gratitude, a foundational aspect of ikigai. Also, permit yourself to appreciate yourself. Ensure you recognize your achievements as often as the areas you need to work on.

Reflective Questions

What daily activities bring you comfort, joy, or peace?

Do specific sensory experiences (smells, sounds, textures) make you happy?

What moments in the past week made you feel a sense of ease or contentment?

Practical Exercise: "Sensory Mapping"

Sensory mapping involves focusing on each of your senses to experience your environment in a deeper, more conscious way. This technique helps shift focus to the physical and sensory world, promoting presence.

How to Practice: Take 10 minutes each day to focus on one sense at a time. Begin by paying attention to sounds, noting background noises or silence around you. Next, shift to sight, observing your surroundings' colors, shapes, and light. Move through touch, smell, and taste, savoring each sensory detail.

Example: Claire, a busy teacher and mother, practices sensory mapping during her lunch break. By focusing on the taste and texture of her meal or the sounds in her environment, she creates a pocket of calm in her day, helping her appreciate her surroundings with fresh awareness.

Practical Exercise: "Gratitude Moments"

This exercise encourages taking short pauses throughout the day to note and appreciate small moments of joy, cultivating gratitude and enhancing mindfulness.

How to Practice: Set an hourly reminder on your phone to express gratitude. When the reminder sounds, take a deep breath, look around, and find something to appreciate—a plant, a person, or simply the warmth of sunlight through a window. Consciously acknowledging these small joys can enhance daily satisfaction.

Example: Ethan, the graphic designer who often worries about the future, finds it grounding to take gratitude moments every few hours. Each pause reminds him to appreciate small comforts, like his cozy workspace or the coffee at his side, helping him feel more present and less anxious.

"Enjoy the little things in life, for one day you will look back and realize they were big things."

— **Robert Brault**

2. Finding Harmony: Exercises to Foster Connection and Balance

Harmony involves creating balance in relationships, routines, and personal habits. In Japanese culture, this concept, known as wa, promotes respect, empathy, and interconnectedness, reminding us that our purpose is often found in relationships with others and the world around us.

Reflective Questions

Which relationships in your life feel supportive and nurturing?

Are any interactions or environments creating a sense of peace and connection?

How can you contribute to a more harmonious atmosphere in your surroundings?

Practical Exercise: "Active Listening Meditation"

Active listening is a mindfulness technique that deepens connections by encouraging us to be fully present in conversations. This exercise fosters harmony by enhancing empathy, respect, and understanding in relationships.

How to Practice: In your following conversation, focus on fully listening without preparing a response or interrupting. Pay attention to the speaker's words, tone, and body language. If you're on the phone, focus on their tone and pauses. Respond thoughtfully, based on what you've honestly heard rather than on assumptions.

Example: Lucas, the digital nomad, often feels isolated working remotely. Practicing active listening during his calls with friends and family helps him connect more deeply, bringing a sense of harmony to his relationships even when he's far away.

Practical Exercise: "Environmental Reset"

Our surroundings can profoundly affect our inner harmony. This exercise involves intentionally creating a peaceful environment to encourage balance and harmony.

How to Practice: Spend 15 minutes each evening tidying or organizing a part of your space, creating a harmonious, uncluttered atmosphere. Place calming objects nearby, like a plant, candle, or photo that brings joy. This small ritual of organizing can foster a sense of balance and tranquility.

Example: Claire, whose workdays can feel hectic, resets her environment each evening before bed. By organizing her kitchen or setting out her work items, she creates a sense of balance, which helps her start each day feeling grounded and prepared.

"Balance is not something you find; it's something you create."

— **Jana Kingsford**

3. Living in the Present: Techniques for Deepening Presence

Mindfulness practices are invaluable tools for calming an overactive mind and paving the way for Zen Clarity—a state of purposeful calmness and focus. Practicing mindfulness can disrupt these negative spirals, nurture calm, and foster Zen Clarity in the present moment. These methods align with the Japanese philosophies of mushin (no-mind) and zazen (seated meditation), encouraging focus, clarity, and peace.

Zen Clarity emerges when we create space for mindfulness in our daily routines. Techniques like mindful walking or zazen calm the mind and reveal pathways to inner peace and purposeful living.

1. The 5-4-3-2-1 Grounding Technique

This simple yet effective method uses your senses to anchor you to the present moment, reducing anxiety and racing thoughts.

Steps:

1. Acknowledge 5 Things You Can See: Look around and identify five items in your surroundings. Notice their colors, shapes, or textures.

2. Acknowledge 4 Things You Can Feel: Pay attention to physical sensations, like the fabric of your clothing, the chair under you, or the breeze on your skin.

3. Acknowledge 3 Things You Can Hear: Listen closely to ambient sounds—birds chirping, the hum of a fan, or distant voices.

4. Acknowledge 2 Things You Can Smell: Focus on scents in the air. If nothing is noticeable, find something nearby, like a cup of tea or an essential oil.

5. Acknowledge 1 Thing You Can Taste: Take a sip of water, chew gum, or notice the lingering taste in your mouth.

This technique helps shift your focus from internal thoughts to the external world, grounding you in the here and now.

2. Progressive Muscle Relaxation

This technique systematically relaxes your body by tensing and releasing each muscle group, promoting physical and mental relaxation. By first tensing the muscles, you heighten your awareness of the contrast between tension and relaxation, allowing the release to be much more effective than simply attempting to relax without this preparation.

Steps:

1. Find a quiet place where you can sit or lie comfortably.

2. Close your eyes and take a few deep breaths, focusing on breathing.

3. Start with your toes. Tense the muscles for 5-7 seconds, then release for 10-15 seconds. Notice the difference between tension and relaxation.

4. Gradually move upward through your body: calves, thighs, abdomen, chest, arms, hands, shoulders, and face.

5. As you release each area, silently repeat a calming affirmation, such as:

"I am letting go of tension."

"I am safe and relaxed."

"I deserve peace."

This practice helps identify and release physical tension while calming the mind.

3. Body Scan Meditation

A body scan is a mindfulness practice that brings awareness to each part of your body, fostering relaxation and connection to the present.

Steps:

1. Lie down or sit comfortably in a quiet space.

2. Close your eyes and take a few deep breaths.

3. Begin at the top of your head, focusing on any sensations you feel. Slowly move your attention downward—your face, neck, shoulders, arms, chest, abdomen, legs, and feet.

4. If you notice tension or discomfort, breathe into that area and silently repeat:

"I release what no longer serves me."

"I welcome calm and peace."

Spend 10-15 minutes on the practice, finishing with a few deep breaths and a moment of gratitude for your body.

5. Zazen (Seated Meditation)

Rooted in Zen Buddhism, zazen is a practice of quiet sitting and mindfulness. It's a foundational technique for developing focus and reducing overthinking.

Steps:

1. Find a comfortable sitting position on a cushion or chair. Keep your back straight and hands resting in your lap.

2. Gently close your eyes or keep them slightly open with a soft gaze.

3. Focus on your breath. Count each exhalation up to 8, then start over. If your mind wanders, gently bring your attention back to your breath.

Practice for 10-20 minutes, gradually increasing the duration as you become more comfortable.

Zazen cultivates a state of calm and acceptance, helping you observe your thoughts without judgment.

6. **Visualization Practice: A Calming Sanctuary**

This exercise uses imagination to create a peaceful mental retreat.

Steps:

1. Sit comfortably and close your eyes.

2. Visualize a serene place like a beach, forest, or cozy room. Focus on the details—colors, sounds, and textures.

3. Imagine yourself there, feeling safe and relaxed. Notice how the air feels, what you hear, and the emotions the space evokes.

4. Silently repeat affirmations such as:

"This is my place of peace."

"I carry this calm with me."

Return to this visualization whenever you feel overwhelmed.

Modern Applications of Mindfulness for a Busy Life

Mindfulness doesn't have to require extensive time or unique settings. Here, we explore brief, accessible exercises suited to modern life that can be incorporated into daily routines, even for those with tight schedules.

Single-Task Focus

Though common, multitasking often reduces our engagement with each activity. Practicing single-task focus allows us to give full attention to one task at a time, enhancing quality and presence.

How to Practice: Choose one activity each day to perform with complete focus. Whether writing an email, cooking a meal, or cleaning, focus on the action without letting your mind wander. Engage your senses as you work, bringing attention to the physical sensations, sounds, and sights involved.

Example: For Rachel, the project manager who frequently juggles tasks, practicing single-task focus is a way to reclaim presence. When writing a project proposal, she closes all other tabs, silences notifications, and dedicates 20 minutes to engage in the task, fully experiencing newfound clarity.

Mindful Walking

Walking meditation is a simple, accessible way to incorporate mindfulness into daily life. This exercise involves walking slowly and deliberately, focusing on each step and creating a deep connection with the present moment.

How to Practice: Set aside 10–15 minutes to walk indoors or outdoors. Walk slowly, paying attention to the sensation of your feet touching the ground, your breath's rhythm, and your body's movement. If thoughts arise, gently bring your focus back to the physical experience of walking.

Example: Ethan, who struggles with anxiety about future projects, takes a mindful walk each morning. Focusing on his steps and the sounds around him makes him calm before starting his workday, helping him stay present and reduce worry.

"Walk as if you are kissing the Earth with your feet."

— **Thich Nhat Hanh**

Mindfulness Micro-Breaks

Micro-breaks are short, intentional pauses during the day that allow for a reset of focus and energy. These breaks bring immediate presence and can be seamlessly integrated into work routines or personal activities.

How to Practice: Set an alarm to take a micro-break every 90 minutes. During each break, close your eyes, take three deep breaths, and focus on releasing tension. Use this moment to reconnect with your physical surroundings and breathe mindfully before returning to your activities.

Example: Lucas often works long hours as a digital nomad and sets his timer for micro-breaks. These brief pauses help him clear his mind and reduce fatigue, enhancing productivity and mindfulness during his workday.

Screen-Free Meal

Eating mindfully encourages presence and enhances our appreciation of flavors and textures, reducing the distractions of screens or rushed eating.

How to Practice: For one meal daily, sit down without your phone or computer. Focus on the taste, texture, and aroma of each bite. Engage fully in the experience of eating, noticing your body's hunger and fullness cues.

Example: Claire usually eats lunch while planning lessons and commits to a screen-free lunch. She finds that eating mindfully boosts her afternoon energy and leaves her feeling more satisfied and less rushed. Although it may seem like taking extra time to eat mindfully, she realizes she doesn't lose time overall; her increased energy and focus make her far more productive and efficient throughout the rest of her day.

Reflection Questions:

Which mindfulness practice did you find most effective in calming your mind? Why?

Have you considered incorporating creative activities, like coloring, into your mindfulness practice? Explore resources such as *Mindfulness Quotes and Coloring Patterns for Mothers* to bring calm and focus to your daily life.

What moments of joy or beauty did you notice while practicing mindfulness in your daily life?

How did being present impact your interactions with others or your focus on tasks?

What changes would you like to make to be more present daily?

Integrating Mindfulness and Ikigai: Creating a Mindful Routine

Once you have uncovered your ikigai—the elements that bring meaning and satisfaction to your life—the next step is learning how to integrate it into your daily routine. Embedding ikigai into everyday life isn't just about knowing what you're passionate about or what contributes to the world; it's about living in alignment with those values in every aspect of your day.

Integrating mindfulness to support ikigai involves creating a simple, repeatable, mindful routine to maintain consistency. A mindful routine doesn't require a significant time commitment but is designed to ground each day, enhancing awareness and gratitude in every action.

How to Practice: Design a daily routine that includes three mindful activities. For example, a morning practice could include (1) a few minutes of deep breathing, (2) mindful coffee or tea preparation and savoring, and (3) a brief gratitude reflection. Aim to repeat these activities daily, observing how they bring focus, calm, and a sense of purpose. Take at least 21 days to introduce a new habit.

Example: the project manager, Rachel, incorporates a mindful morning routine. She starts her day with breathing exercises, makes her coffee slowly while focusing on the aroma, and ends by noting three things she's grateful for. This routine supports her focus and helps her start each day grounded and purpose-driven.

When ikigai becomes part of our habits, it will help automate our tasks, reducing the mental load of constantly making decisions. This alignment simplifies life and nurtures Zen Clarity, allowing us to live with focused intention and ease. Establishing simple, consistent routines frees up mental space, making it easier to focus on more important choices and actions aligned with your ikigai.

This section will cover strategies for aligning actions with purpose.

Morning Intentions: Starting the Day with Purpose

Starting your day with a brief intention-setting practice can be a powerful way to align your actions with your ikigai from the beginning. This can involve reflecting on your purpose, setting goals that align with your values, or simply focusing on qualities you want to bring into your interactions.

How to Practice Morning Intentions

Identify a Daily Intention: When you wake up, reflect on your purpose or something meaningful you want to accomplish that day. This intention can be broad, like "I will approach my work with compassion," or specific, like "I will complete my project with patience and care."

Link Intentions to Ikigai: For example, if your ikigai involves teaching, your intention could be to bring patience and encouragement to your students that day. This mental link between your ikigai and your daily activities fosters a mindset that finds purpose in even routine tasks.

Example: Rachel, the project manager, intends to approach her day empathetically, aligning with her ikigai of mentoring and guiding others. Each morning, she reflects on how she can support her team and create a collaborative environment, helping her feel fulfilled even on busy days.

"Each day is a journey, and the journey itself is home."

— **Matsuo Basho**

Prioritizing Tasks with Ikigai

Traditional planning methods sometimes feel transactional, focusing on task completion rather than purpose. Purposeful planning is a way to integrate ikigai into your work by prioritizing tasks that align with your values, focusing on projects that contribute meaningfully, and incorporating breaks that allow for reflection and realignment.

How to Practice Purposeful Planning

Prioritize Meaningful Tasks: At the beginning of each week, identify tasks or projects that resonate most with your ikigai. If your ikigai involves creativity, prioritize tasks that allow for creative expression. If it's helping others, focus on projects that contribute to those around you.

Add Reflection Breaks: Plan short breaks during the day to reassess and ensure you're working in alignment with your ikigai. This keeps your intentions fresh and helps reduce stress by allowing regular checks on your focus and mindset. Knowing you'll have a dedicated moment to review and make adjustments at the end reduces the urge to overthink or constantly edit while working. As a result, you can concentrate more fully on the task at hand, boosting efficiency and focus.

Example: Lucas, the digital nomad, uses purposeful planning to balance his work and personal life, which supports his ikigai of finding freedom and creativity. He ensures that he dedicates time to client work and personal projects each week, helping him feel fulfilled and aligned with his purpose.

Engaging Fully with Each Task

Incorporating ikigai into daily routines means transforming simple, routine tasks into mindful actions. By engaging fully with each activity and performing it with intention, you bring purpose to tasks that might otherwise feel mundane. This approach enhances productivity and cultivates joy and satisfaction in daily life.

Practical exercises

Focus on One Thing at a Time: Multitasking dilutes attention and can increase stress. Focusing on a single task allows you to engage more deeply, bringing quality and presence to each action. If your ikigai is about bringing beauty into the world, try to find the aesthetic or positive in whatever you are doing.

Find Meaning in Small Actions: For tasks that seem unrelated to your ikigai, find ways to connect them. For example, if you're passionate about helping others but find yourself doing solitary work, remind yourself that your efforts contribute indirectly to a larger purpose or those around you.

Example: Ethan, the graphic designer incorporates his ikigai of creative expression into each project. Rather than rushing through tasks, he treats each design as an opportunity to express his creativity, bringing a sense of purpose to his work, even on routine assignments.

"The way to find purpose is to put your whole heart into every task, no matter how small."

— **Japanese Proverb**

Practicing Gratitude and Reflection in the evening

Ending the day with gratitude and reflection helps reinforce ikigai by recognizing the positive aspects of daily experiences. Evening reflection enhances life satisfaction and serves as a mental reset, helping to reduce overthinking by focusing on accomplishments rather than worries.

How to Practice Evening Reflection

Reflect on Purposeful Actions: At the end of each day, remember moments where you felt connected to your ikigai. What tasks brought satisfaction? Were there interactions that aligned with your values? This reflection fosters awareness of purpose and encourages self-appreciation.

Identify Growth Areas: Recognize moments where you could improve or actions didn't fully align with your purpose. By viewing these moments as opportunities for growth, you can adjust to living in better alignment with your ikigai moving forward.

Example: Claire, the teacher, reflects each evening on how she supported her students and whether her actions aligned with her ikigai of fostering educational equality. This practice brings her peace and a sense of achievement, reinforcing her purpose as she plans for the next day.

"Reflection is the lamp that lights the way for our future."

— **Japanese Proverb**

Building Connections that Reflect Your Ikigai

Our relationships play a crucial role in sustaining ikigai, as they provide support, inspiration, and opportunities for growth. Connecting with people who share or respect your values strengthens your purpose and brings harmony. Equally important is recognizing and minimizing interactions with those who drain your energy, criticize, or impose their expectations on you. Surrounding yourself with positive, uplifting influences helps maintain your focus and motivation, allowing your ikigai to flourish without unnecessary stress or doubt.

How to Build Purposeful Connections

Seek Out Like-Minded Individuals: Engage in communities or groups where you can connect with others with similar interests, goals, or values. Whether it's a professional network, hobby group, or local organization, being around like-minded people can reinforce your commitment to ikigai.

Strengthen Existing Bonds: Share your ikigai with close friends or family members, letting them know what fulfills you. Invite them to participate in activities that align with your purposes, such as volunteering, creative projects, or fitness routines.

Example: Lucas builds connections with fellow remote workers, finding camaraderie with people who understand his lifestyle and values. These relationships help him feel supported and reinforce his ikigai of creating a flexible, freedom-based life.

Creating a Restorative Environment

The Zen idea of "return home and find peace" highlights the importance of our personal space as a sanctuary for rest and renewal. In our busy, overcommitted lives, it's easy to overlook the role of our environment in shaping our mental and emotional well-being. Yet, a calming, intentional space can provide the foundation for quieting the mind and reconnecting with ourselves.

The Purpose of Your Space

Your space doesn't need to be perfect or filled with expensive objects to serve as a place of restoration. The goal is not to embark on a home improvement project or add more items to your to-do list. Instead, think of your personal space as a tool for mindfulness and self-care—a retreat from the busyness of the outside world.

Ask yourself: Does your environment support your need for relaxation, clarity, and presence? Consider how small adjustments might transform your space into a haven of calm.

How to Cultivate a Peaceful Atmosphere

Declutter with Purpose: Start by removing items that don't contribute to your goal of rest and relaxation. Clutter can be a physical reminder of undone tasks, creating unnecessary mental noise. Let go of what no longer serves you—this is not about minimalism for its own sake but about making room for peace.

Focus on Atmosphere, Not Objects: Rather than filling your space with things marketed as "relaxing," create a soothing atmosphere. This might mean introducing soft lighting, incorporating a few natural elements like plants or stones, or arranging furniture to promote openness and flow. The emphasis should be on how the space feels rather than how it looks.

Define Your Restful Space: Designate a small area for unwinding, such as a cozy chair by a window or a quiet corner with a comfortable mat or cushion. Use this space intentionally for activities like reading, meditation, or pausing to reflect.

Example: Claire, our creative teacher, often found herself overwhelmed by the demands of her workday. Inspired by the idea of a restorative environment, she created a simple corner in her living room. She placed a comfortable chair by the window, added a small plant, and lit a candle in the evenings. This corner became her sanctuary—a space where she could journal, breathe deeply, and let the day's stress melt away. The simplicity of the space helped her connect with her ikigai by providing a calm, intentional environment to reflect and recharge.

Your personal space is an extension of your inner world. Creating a restorative environment invites peace and mindfulness into your life, helping to quiet overthinking and reconnect with your purpose. Remember, it's not about perfection but crafting a space that feels like home for your soul—a place to breathe, unwind, and simply be.

Using ikigai as a Guide in Decision-Making

Integrating ikigai into decision-making processes can reduce stress and overthinking by providing a clear framework for choices. Making decisions based on your ikigai makes you feel more confident and content with the outcomes, even if they involve challenges.

How to Use Ikigai in Decision-Making

Consider Each Element of Ikigai: When faced with a decision, evaluate how it aligns with what you love, what you're good at, what the world needs, and what you can be paid for. This evaluation offers a balanced perspective that aligns with personal and practical needs.

Visualize Long-Term Alignment: Consider how the decision will support or hinder your ikigai in the long run. Does it bring you closer to the life you envision for yourself, or does it detract from it? This foresight helps you stay true to your purpose.

Reflect and Act: A good way to motivate yourself to make a necessary decision is to reflect on your significant choices and analyze their impact on your life. This exercise can offer valuable insights into how confident choices shape your path. Now, write down the decisions you need to make, and next to each one, note the positive outcomes you expect. This practice clarifies your options and encourages you to take action by focusing on the potential benefits of your choices.

Example: Rachel is considering a job change. She feels more confident about her decision by evaluating how the new role aligns with her ikigai of mentoring others. Although the role involves challenges, knowing it fulfills her ikigai reassures her that it's the right choice.

"When decisions align with purpose, life becomes clearer and more fulfilling."

— **Anonymous**

Focusing on What Matters: The Wisdom of Shouganai

In our rapidly changing environment and overthinking-prone lives, getting stuck on things we can't control or feel missing is easy. The Japanese concept of shouganai—loosely translated as "it cannot be helped"—asks us to accept what is beyond our control and focus on what we can influence. This doesn't mean giving up or resigning to fate. Instead, a practical mindset encourages us to shift our energy toward meaningful action and release the mental clutter that drains us.

Shouganai aligns beautifully with other Japanese philosophies, such as wabi-sabi, which embraces the beauty of imperfection, and kaizen, which focuses on small, deliberate steps toward improvement. Together, these principles guide us to reframe our thinking and center our attention on what truly matters.

Here are four powerful shifts in mindset, inspired by these Japanese philosophies, that can help quiet overthinking and align your actions with your ikigai:

Control What You Can, Let Go of What You Can't: One of the first steps in reducing overthinking is recognizing the difference between what you can control and what you cannot. Worrying about things outside your influence only drains your energy and perpetuates mental spirals. Shouganai helps us to accept gracefully what is unchangeable and redirect our focus to areas where we can make a difference.

Practical Tip:

- **Make two lists:** one for things you can control and one for things you can't.
- **Choose one item from the "can control" list** and take a concrete step toward resolving it, no matter how small.
- **For items on the "cannot control" list**, consciously release them by reminding yourself, *shouganai*—it cannot be helped.

Focus on What You Can Do, Not What You Can't: Overthinking often traps us in the impossible, feeling stuck and powerless. Instead, shift your attention to what you can achieve. Even a small action can break the cycle of inaction and create a sense of progress. This aligns with the philosophy of kaizen, which emphasizes incremental improvement and steady growth.

Practical Tip:

When faced with an overwhelming situation, ask yourself:

- **Act immediately:** "What is one thing I can do right now to move forward?" Even small steps can reframe the problem and redirect your focus to actionable solutions rather than obstacles.

Example: When Claire felt overwhelmed by a large work project, she focused on drafting just the first paragraph of her report. Completing this small task-built momentum, helping her move forward with confidence.

Focus on What You Have, Not What You Don't: It's human nature to dwell on what we lack, whether material possessions, skills, or opportunities. This perspective fuels dissatisfaction and overthinking. The philosophy of wabi-sabi encourages us to find beauty and contentment in what we already have, no matter how imperfect or incomplete it may seem.

Practical Tip:

- **Begin a gratitude practice.** Each evening, list three things you're grateful for, no matter how small or imperfect they may seem. Reflect on how these things contribute to your life and what they reveal about your priorities.

Focus on What You Need, Not Just What You Want: Chasing every desire can lead to frustration and exhaustion. Instead, prioritize what you truly need—physically, emotionally, and mentally. Shouganai reminds us that we can't have everything we want. Still, we can find fulfillment by focusing on what is essential. Practical Tip:

- **Check if something is essential:** When faced with a decision, ask yourself, "Is this something I truly need, or is it a fleeting want?" Focus on fulfilling what's essential and aligning your energy with what genuinely matters.

Overthinking often thrives on what we can't control, don't have, or wish were different. Shouganai helps us shift our focus to what we can control, what we can do, what we already have, and what we truly need; we simplify our mental landscape and bring greater clarity to our lives. These mindset shifts are practical and deeply transformative, helping us align with our ikigai and live with purpose and peace.

Creating a Personal Ikigai Manifesto

A personal manifesto is a written declaration of your purpose, values, and goals, constantly reminding you of your ikigai. By crafting a manifesto, you create a guiding document that reinforces your daily purpose and keeps you focused on what truly matters.

How to Create an Ikigai Manifesto

Write Down Your Purpose Statement: Begin with a simple statement of your ikigai. It could be something like, "My purpose is to bring creativity and empathy into the world through my interactions and work."

List Core Values and Goals: Outline the values you want to embody and the goals that support your ikigai. These include traits like kindness, resilience, and generosity, as well as specific aspirations like learning a new skill or volunteering regularly.

Review Regularly: Place your manifesto somewhere visible and review it daily or weekly. This regular reminder keeps you grounded in your ikigai and ensures that your actions align with your purpose.

Example: Graphic designer Ethan writes his ikigai manifesto to ground his daily work purposefully. Each morning, he revisits it while setting a small, achievable goal. His manifesto reads, "My purpose is to use design to communicate meaningful ideas and help clients clearly express their visions." He paired this with a weekly ritual of setting small goals, like networking with potential clients. This approach restored his confidence and built a steady client base within months.

A personal manifesto not only reminds us of our purpose but also grounds decision-making in values, creating a sense of direction in both professional and personal life. While a personal ikigai statement identifies what brings meaning and joy, a manifesto expands upon this by outlining specific principles and actionable commitments to live by. The manifesto becomes a tool for alignment, reducing stress by providing a clear framework for daily choices and actions and as a constant reference point for navigating challenges and opportunities with clarity.

Give your Ikigai Manifesto a Name

Naming your manifesto is a creative and empowering way to solidify your purpose. A thoughtfully chosen title can remind you daily of your aspirations and values, guiding you with clarity and focus. The name doesn't have to be elaborate—it just needs to resonate deeply with you and reflect your personal journey.

Here are some inspiring examples to help you find the perfect name for your manifesto:

1. Inspired by Growth and Transformation

- "The Blossoming Path" Evokes the beauty of gradual growth and is perfect for those seeking personal and professional transformation.
- "Steps to the Summit": A motivational title for those tackling big goals, one step at a time.
- "The Phoenix Blueprint": For individuals rising stronger from setbacks, embodying resilience and renewal.

2. Rooted in Peace and Balance

- "Harmony Within": Reflecting a journey toward inner calm and balance.
- "The Still Waters Guide": A poetic nod to mindfulness and clarity in chaos.
- "Serenity in Motion": Ideal for those balancing dynamic lives with moments of stillness.

3. Focused on Contribution and Legacy

- "Echoes of Purpose": Highlighting the ripple effect of your meaningful actions on others.
- "The Lightkeeper's Map": For those guiding others while staying true to their path.
- "A Thousand Hands": Representing a mission of service and connection to the greater good.

4. Energized by Creativity and Passion

- "Canvas of Dreams": A title for artists and dreamers bringing their visions to life.
- "Symphony of Joy": For those whose ikigai revolves around creating happiness for themselves and others.
- "Flames of Creation": Representing the fiery passion that fuels innovative minds.

Tips for Choosing Your Manifesto's Name

- **Keep it Personal**: The name should resonate with your unique ikigai journey.
- **Think Symbolically**: Use metaphors or imagery that inspire you.
- **Stay Open to Change**: As your ikigai evolves, don't hesitate to revisit and refine the title.

Your manifesto's name is more than a label—it reflects your aspirations and the guiding light on your journey. Take the time to choose a name that uplifts and motivates you daily, reminding you of your purpose and potential.

Embracing Flexibility: Allowing Ikigai to Evolve

While ikigai provides a sense of direction, it's also essential to allow flexibility as life circumstances, interests, and personal growth evolve. Embracing flexibility in your ikigai provides a resilient sense of purpose that adapts over time.

How to Practice Flexibility with Ikigai

Regular Check-Ins: Revisit your ikigai statement or manifesto every few months to ensure it still resonates. Consider whether certain aspects of your purpose or values have shifted, and adjust your goals accordingly.

Adapt Goals to Current Life Stages: Recognize that ikigai may shift with different life stages. For instance, your ikigai might focus on skill-building and contribution during career growth. At the same time, later life may center on giving back or finding peace in simpler joys.

Example: Claire's passion for educational equity evolved. Once a dedicated classroom teacher, she now envisions a broader impact by mentoring new educators and creating community learning initiatives. This gradual shift allows her to stay connected to her ikigai while embracing new ways of contributing, proving that purpose can grow alongside life's changes.

This flexibility creates resilience, ensuring that your ikigai remains a guiding presence no matter how circumstances change.

Reflection Questions:

Which point in the integration process resonated most with you (e.g., morning intentions, evening gratitude)?

How did aligning your daily tasks with your ikigai shift your perspective or energy levels?

What obstacles did you encounter while applying these practices, and how did you address them?

Which step felt most difficult or unfamiliar, and what support might help you practice it more effectively?

Applying Ikigai in Times of Stress or Challenge

Life inevitably brings periods of stress, uncertainty, and challenge. During such times, ikigai can be a stabilizing anchor, helping you navigate difficulties with a sense of purpose and inner strength.

How to Rely on Ikigai During Challenges

Reconnect with Core Purpose: In moments of stress, return to your ikigai. Reflect on how the current challenge aligns with your larger purpose. This mindset can transform obstacles into meaningful growth experiences, reminding you that each step contributes to your journey, no matter how difficult.

Focus on Meaningful Actions: During difficult times, focus on small actions that bring you closer to your purpose. This approach reduces stress by breaking down overwhelming tasks and helps you stay rooted in what matters most.

Example: Rachel, facing the pressures of a high-stakes project, rediscovered her ikigai through mentorship. Instead of succumbing to stress, she shifted her focus to empowering her team by offering guidance and celebrating small wins. This renewed sense of purpose eased her stress and improved team morale, showing her that growth comes from shared success rather than personal perfection.

Integrating ikigai in adversity creates resilience, helping one maintain perspective and remain grounded.

Setting Boundaries

Setting boundaries is not just about saying "no" but creating space for what truly matters. For many, the inability to set boundaries leads to overcommitment, stress, and overthinking. By defining clear limits, we honor our time, energy, and purpose—key elements of living an ikigai-aligned life.

Why Setting Boundaries Matters

Boundaries protect your focus and emotional energy. They can prevent you from drifting into obligations that do not align with your values or ikigai. This can lead to frustration, burnout, and a sense of being unmoored from your purpose. Boundaries also reduce decision fatigue by clarifying your priorities.

Practical tips:

Identify Your Limits: Reflect on what drains your energy and what replenishes it. Write down tasks, relationships, or commitments that align with your ikigai and those that don't. Use this list to identify areas where boundaries are needed.

> **Example:** If attending every social event leaves you exhausted, limit how many events you participate in a month, focusing instead on those that bring you joy or align with your goals.

Communicate Clearly and Compassionately: Boundaries are not walls; they are agreements. When setting a boundary, express it with clarity and kindness.

> **Example:** Instead of saying, "I'm too busy to help," try, "I'm focusing on personal goals right now and need to prioritize my time. Thank you for understanding."

Create Time for Yourself: Carve out regular periods of solitude or self-care. This might mean scheduling "quiet hours" or turning down non-essential obligations.

Example: Dedicate the first hour of your day to activities like journaling, meditation, or exercise that align with your ikigai.

Practice Mindful Awareness: Use mindfulness techniques to recognize when you feel stretched too thin. Emotional signals like frustration or overwhelm often indicate a need for firmer boundaries.

In Japanese culture, harmony (wa) and balance are deeply valued. Setting boundaries may initially seem contrary to these ideals. Still, it is a way to preserve inner harmony and align with your ikigai. Boundaries help manage overthinking and overwhelming feelings by allowing you to focus your energy on what truly matters—those activities, relationships, and responsibilities that resonate with your purpose.

How Japanese Concepts Support Boundary Setting

Japanese wisdom emphasizes balance and intentionality, both of which are foundational to setting boundaries:

- **Shouganai (It Can't Be Helped)**: This philosophy encourages accepting what you can't control and focusing energy on what you can. With the help of *shouganai*, you can release guilt over saying no to things beyond your capacity. Saying no can sometimes feel uncomfortable, especially when you want to meet others' expectations. Adopting shouganai allows us to accept our limitations with grace, leading to an understanding that we cannot do everything for everyone without depleting ourselves.

- **Mushin (No-Mind)**: Practicing *mushin* helps you let go of overanalyzing and act on what aligns with your purpose. This reduces the mental clutter that makes boundary-setting difficult. You can objectively assess requests or demands by cultivating a calm and focused mind. This clarity helps you identify what aligns with your purpose and detracts from it.

- **Wabi-Sabi**: Embracing imperfection reminds us that we don't need to do everything or please everyone to lead a meaningful life.

- **Maintaining Inner Harmony:** Concepts like *ma* (space) remind us of the importance of pauses and balance. Creating boundaries allows you to introduce moments of stillness, ensuring you don't overcommit and lose sight of your ikigai.

The Impact of Boundaries on Overthinking

Without boundaries, competing demands constantly bombard the mind, leading to decision fatigue and overthinking. Setting clear limits simplifies choices and allows you to focus on actions that bring joy, fulfillment, and purpose.

A Practical Exercise for Boundary-Setting

1. List three areas of your life where you feel overwhelmed or unfulfilled.
2. For each area, identify one boundary you can set.

3. Write a simple, compassionate script for communicating this boundary to others.
4. Reflect on how these boundaries support your ikigai and emotional well-being.

Boundaries are not selfish; they're essential to leading a purposeful life. By protecting your time and energy, you create space for what truly matters, bringing you closer to your ikigai and reducing the stress of overthinking.

How to Set Boundaries Mindfully

Anchor Your Decisions in Ikigai: Before agreeing to a request or commitment, ask yourself: Does this align with what I love, what I'm good at, what the world needs, or what sustains me financially? If not, it may be better to decline.

Create Space with Small Changes: Begin with simple, manageable steps to reduce overwhelm. For example, reserve blocks of time in your day for rest or reflection and learn to decline requests that encroach on this space politely. Over time, these boundaries will help you protect your energy and focus.

Example: Ethan, a busy freelancer, struggled to manage client demands, often saying yes to every project out of fear of losing work. This left him overwhelmed and unable to focus on the parts of his work he truly enjoyed. Reflecting on his ikigai, he realized that quality mattered more than quantity. He politely turned down projects that didn't align with his strengths or interests. This shift reduced his stress and allowed him to deliver better results on the projects he valued most.

Boundary setting is a vital tool for maintaining harmony within yourself and staying true to your ikigai. By respectfully saying no to what doesn't serve your purpose, you create space for clarity, focus, and fulfillment. Remember, every thoughtful no is a step closer to living a life aligned with your values and priorities.

Overthinking in Relationships: Building Healthy Boundaries

Overthinking often affects how we relate to others. Emotional boundaries help avoid overanalyzing relationships and create space for authentic interactions:

- **Clarify Intentions:** Instead of assuming, ask. A simple question can prevent hours of overthinking.
- **Communicate Your Needs:** Share your feelings rather than letting others guess your emotions. This reduces the strain of miscommunication.
- **Practice Mindfulness in Interactions:** Being present with others helps you engage fully and avoids overthinking what's left unsaid.

Establishing boundaries within relationships encourages trust and reduces the mental clutter caused by overanalyzing others' actions or feelings.

Finding Ikigai When You Feel Stuck

Ikigai can help you get unstuck by providing direction and clarity, even when life feels overwhelming or stagnant. You can break free from inertia by reflecting on the elements of ikigai and taking small steps toward alignment.

Life sometimes puts us in limiting situations where it seems impossible to follow our passions or use our talents. However, even in these moments, you can shift your perspective to align your current reality with your sense of purpose.

Steps to Align Your Ikigai

1. Start from "What the World Needs"

If you can't pursue what you love or excel at right now, focus on the immediate needs around you. Identify how you can contribute meaningfully, even if it's not your ideal role, and find satisfaction in serving others.

Practical Tip: Make a list of ways you can meet the needs of your community, workplace, or family. Look for opportunities to serve and connect, even by small gestures.

Example: Claire, a teacher overwhelmed by administrative tasks, shifts her mindset by focusing on her students' needs. Instead of feeling trapped, she finds fulfillment in moments where she can positively impact their lives.

2. Cultivate Meaning in Small Actions

Embrace the traditional ikigai approach by finding purpose in daily tasks, no matter how small. Align your actions with your core values and let go of the expectation that everything must be perfect or passion-driven.

Practical Tip: Identify one daily task you can approach with mindfulness and intention. Whether cooking a meal, organizing your workspace, or helping a colleague, view it as an opportunity to make a difference.

Example: Kevin, a graphic designer, felt uninspired by routine projects. By creating designs that resonate emotionally with clients, he found renewed purpose in his work, even in small assignments.

3. Adjust Your Perspective on Setbacks

Life's unexpected turns can feel like obstacles, but they also present opportunities to grow and adapt. Reframing challenges as part of your ikigai journey can help you stay connected to your values and goals.

Practical Tip: Reflect on past setbacks and identify lessons or skills you gained. Write about how these experiences align with your broader purpose.

Example: Samantha, who was laid off from her corporate job, used the opportunity to volunteer at a local non-profit. This experience helped her discover a new passion for community work, reshaping her ikigai.

4. Incorporate Flexibility into Your Path

Your ikigai is not fixed—it evolves as you grow and your circumstances change. By being flexible, you open yourself to new opportunities and redefine purpose as needed.

Practical Tip: Create a personal "Ikigai check-in" every six months. Reflect on how your actions align with your values and goals, and adjust your path if needed.

Even when life doesn't go as planned, we can find purpose by adapting our mindset and aligning with the present needs around us. Doing so creates a meaningful path, no matter the circumstances. Remember, ikigai is not about perfection—it's about living intentionally and finding joy in growth and contribution.

Reflection Questions:

What current responsibilities or life circumstances do you feel like they limit your ability to pursue your ikigai?

How can you reframe these situations to connect with "what the world needs" or other elements of ikigai?

What small steps can you take to find meaning or fulfillment even in less-than-ideal circumstances?

Who or what could support you as you navigate this challenging period?

Building Resilience and Adaptability Through Ikigai

Emotional stability lies at the core of resilience. It's the ability to maintain inner calm and balance in adversity. The Japanese philosophies of gaman (endurance) and ganbaru (perseverance) cultivate this emotional foundation, making us remain composed and steady even when life feels uncertain. These practices strengthen our capacity to adapt while staying true to our ikigai.

Life is full of unexpected challenges, and resilience—the ability to recover and adapt—is a skill that helps us navigate these moments with strength and clarity. Ikigai, when combined with complementary Japanese philosophies like gaman (endurance) and ganbaru (perseverance), offers a framework for developing this resilience. These concepts remind us that purpose and persistence can guide us forward even in difficult times, helping us endure and thrive.

Cultivate Inner Strength: Gaman, often translated as "endurance" or "patience," is a Japanese philosophy emphasizing quiet strength in adversity. When life throws you unexpected challenges, practice accepting them with grace and resolve instead of resisting them. For example, if you're facing uncertainty at work or a personal setback, reflect on how this moment fits into your larger ikigai. Focusing on the purpose behind your actions can help you endure difficulties while staying true to your values.

Preserve with Purpose: Ganbaru means to "do your best" or "persist. " It encourages a determined, proactive attitude even when faced with obstacles. Use this mindset to adapt to changing circumstances while staying aligned with your ikigai. When plans fall apart or goals seem out of reach, ganbaru reminds us to adjust, refine, and keep moving forward. Break challenges into smaller, manageable steps, drawing on kaizen principles to stay consistent and focused.

Example: Consider Ethan, a freelancer who experienced a sudden loss of clients due to market changes. At first, the situation felt overwhelming, threatening his sense of purpose and stability. By reflecting on his ikigai, Ethan reminded himself of why he chose freelancing in the first place: his passion for creativity and his desire to make a meaningful impact through his work. Using ganbaru, he restructured his approach, seeking out smaller projects and networking opportunities. He also leaned on gaman, practicing patience and resilience during quieter periods, ultimately allowing him to adapt and rebuild his career on a stronger foundation.

Resilience doesn't mean avoiding hardship—facing challenges with purpose and adaptability, even when negative spirals of doubt or fear threaten to pull you off course. By embracing gaman and ganbaru alongside your ikigai, you can navigate life's unpredictability with strength and grace. Adaptation is not a compromise; it's a powerful skill that allows you to align with your values even in the face of change. Remember, your ikigai is not static—it evolves with you, offering guidance and stability no matter what life brings. Trust in the process, and know that each step forward, no matter how small, builds resilience for the journey ahead.

Self-Compassion: The Foundation of Mindfulness and Resilience

Self-compassion is a powerful tool that bridges mindfulness and resilience, allowing us to navigate life's challenges with greater ease and kindness toward ourselves. While traditional Japanese culture often emphasizes perseverance (ganbaru) and endurance (gaman), these concepts don't preclude the importance of self-compassion. They can be enriched by treating oneself with care and understanding, particularly in moments of difficulty.

In the context of ikigai, self-compassion becomes essential. Living a life of purpose often requires facing uncertainties, adapting to change, and forgiving ourselves when things don't go as planned. It's not about perfection but embracing imperfection with the same grace we extend to others.

The Role of Japanese Wisdom in Self-Compassion

Embracing Imperfection: Wabi-sabi coaches us to find beauty in imperfection and transience. Applying this to ourselves means recognizing that our flaws or failures do not define us. Instead of criticizing ourselves for not meeting unrealistic expectations, we can accept our imperfections as part of our unique journey.

Acceptance of Limitations: Shouganai reminds us that some things are beyond our control. When faced with setbacks or mistakes, shouganai supports us in letting go of guilt and regret, allowing us to focus on what we can do moving forward rather than dwelling on what we cannot change.

Mindfulness and Presence: Mindfulness, closely linked to mushin (no-mind), involves being present at the moment without judgment, gently breaking the cycle of negative spirals that overthinking creates. Self-compassion enhances mindfulness by encouraging us to observe our struggles with curiosity and kindness rather than self-criticism.

Mindfulness practices, like the 5-4-3-2-1 sensory method and zazen meditation, are not just tools for calming the mind but essential for fostering emotional stability. By grounding ourselves in the present moment, we break free from the grip of negative spirals caused by overthinking and create a balanced state of mind. This stability enables us to approach challenges and decisions with clarity, free from the overwhelm of negative spirals. Mindfulness practices like zazen meditation not only ground you in the present but also significantly reduce anxiety by calming the mind and slowing racing thoughts.

How to Practice Self-Compassion

Pause and Reflect: When you feel overwhelmed or self-critical, take a mindful moment to pause. Ask yourself: What would I say to a friend in this situation? Then, offer those same words of encouragement to yourself.

Acknowledge Your Efforts: Celebrate small wins and recognize the effort you've put in, even if the outcome isn't perfect. Practicing kaizen (small, continuous improvement) reminds us that progress is more important than perfection.

Find Solace in Nature: Engage in shinrin-yoku (forest bathing) or other grounding activities to connect with the world around you. These practices can help reset your perspective and remind you that you are part of a larger, ever-changing whole.

Example: Claire, the teacher from earlier chapters, often berated herself for not being able to meet every demand placed on her. Over time, she began integrating self-compassion into her daily mindfulness practice, reminding herself she was doing her best in challenging circumstances. Through wabi-sabi, she found peace in her imperfections, allowing herself to enjoy the process rather than constantly striving for an unattainable ideal.

Self-compassion is not an indulgence—it's a critical component of resilience and mindfulness. By treating ourselves with kindness and understanding, we build the inner strength to face life's challenges and stay aligned with our ikigai. Remember, living a purposeful life begins with extending the same compassion to yourself that you offer to others.

Reflection Questions:

What recent challenge tested your resilience, and how did you respond?

How did practicing gaman (endurance) or ganbaru (perseverance) affect your ability to overcome difficulty?

What habits or practices helped you adapt during moments of uncertainty?

How can you strengthen your ability to balance resilience and self-care in the future?

The Challenges of My Change

Integrating ikigai into my daily life was a process filled with trial and error. One of my most challenging concepts was kaizen—taking small, deliberate steps toward improvement. I had always been an all-or-nothing thinker. If I couldn't tackle a problem in its entirety, I felt like I wasn't trying hard enough and fell into procrastination. Shifting this mindset wasn't easy.

I started small, blocking just 15 minutes daily to reflect on what tasks aligned with my ikigai. At first, it felt insignificant. How could 15 minutes make a difference in a chaotic, overcommitted schedule? But as I stuck with it, I realized that this time allowed me to see patterns in my actions—where I was wasting energy on things that didn't serve my purpose and needed to say no.

Saying no was another hurdle. As someone who always wanted to please others, declining tasks or commitments felt almost impossible. But as I began prioritizing what truly mattered, I noticed something surprising: the people around me started respecting my boundaries. By focusing my time and energy on what aligned with my ikigai, I not only reduced my stress but also created better outcomes in the areas that truly mattered.

Trust the Process: Growth is Gradual and Meaningful

As you reach the end of this book, pause and reflect on the steps you've taken—not just by reading these pages but by opening yourself to the possibility of change. The path to discovering and living your ikigai is not a straight line. It twists and turns, revealing new lessons and challenges at every step. There will be moments when clarity feels elusive and others when everything aligns beautifully, as if life itself is cheering you on.

Your ikigai isn't a single destination or achievement; it's a way of being. It's waking up with purpose and going to bed with gratitude. It's embracing the imperfections, trusting your instincts, and walking your path with curiosity and courage. It's finding joy in the small moments and trusting that they form a larger, more meaningful picture.

Remember, your work so far is a testament to your strength and resilience. You've already proven to yourself that growth is possible. No matter where you are in your journey, choosing to live with intention is a victory. Trust the process, and trust yourself.

Consider keeping a journal where you document your experiences and reflections as you explore ikigai. This journal can serve as a record of your progress, a place to capture insights, and a tool to stay motivated. Over time, you'll be able to look back and see how far you've come, which is a powerful reminder of the value of small, consistent actions.

"Little by little, one travels far."

— **J.R.R. Tolkien**

Sharing Your Journey: Inspire Others and Celebrate Your Progress

From recognizing the negative spirals of overthinking to exploring Japanese wisdom, this book has guided you to understand how small, intentional changes can lead to profound clarity. Whether it's kaizen's incremental steps or ikigai's holistic purpose, these philosophies offer a roadmap to lasting peace. As you continue exploring ikigai and connecting concepts, consider sharing your experiences with others. Talking about your journey not only reinforces your commitment but can also inspire those around you. Sharing ideas, lessons learned, or challenges creates a sense of community. It reminds us that we are not alone in our pursuit of purpose.

If you feel comfortable, share your reflections, insights, or experiences from this book with friends, family, or even online communities. Reviews and comments are valuable ways to connect with like-minded individuals and encourage others to embark on their own journeys. A review on Amazon, where you can express what resonated most with you, is greatly appreciated. Sharing your experience may spark inspiration for someone seeking direction or struggling with overthinking.

Example of Reflection: Imagine Rachel, who writes a review or posts about her journey with ikigai, sharing how the book helped her find new ways to inspire her team and find peace in her work. Her insights might encourage someone else to explore their purpose, creating a ripple effect of positive change.

"By sharing our stories, we find common ground, and in that common ground, we discover a profound sense of belonging."

— **Brené Brown**

The First Step: Taking Action with Intention

You're taking the first step toward breaking free from overthinking and rediscovering purpose. By adopting the principles of ikigai, mindfulness, and acceptance, you've unlocked the tools to transform your life. Now, the journey truly begins.

As you close this book, take these small but meaningful steps:

1. Reflect on your ikigai by journaling about what you love and what the world needs.
2. Practice kaizen by identifying one small change you can make today.
3. Embrace shouganai by letting go of one worry that's beyond your control.

These steps, though simple, are the beginning of a journey that holds the potential to transform your relationship with stress, purpose, and self-acceptance.

Whatever your first step may be, embrace it with an open heart and a willingness to explore. Knowing that every small action can help you climb out of negative spirals and move towards a life of clarity and balance. The path to ikigai is one of curiosity, patience, and growth. Remember, it's not about perfection or rapid progress—it's about being present, valuing each step, and cultivating a life that aligns with who you truly are. Let ikigai guide you forward, one mindful step at a time.

Thank you for allowing this book to be a part of your journey.

Frequently Asked Questions

As you've journeyed through this book, you've explored powerful concepts and practical steps to discover your ikigai, calm overthinking, and create a life aligned with your values. It's natural to have lingering questions—after all, finding purpose and making meaningful changes isn't a one-size-fits-all process. This FAQ section addresses some doubts and curiosities that may arise as you apply these ideas in your own life.

I encourage you to keep reading to find answers and deepen your understanding of how these practices can work for you. As you reflect on these questions, remember that you're not alone on this journey. I, too, started from a place of uncertainty and overthinking, learning through trial and error how to bring clarity and balance into my life.

After the FAQ, I'll share my final reflections—lessons learned, insights gained, and the enduring value of walking this path. I hope my story inspires you to trust your own process, embrace every step forward, and continue exploring the possibilities that ikigai can bring into your life.

Let's dive into your questions together.

1. Does everybody have ikigai?

Yes, everyone has an ikigai, even if it's not immediately apparent. Your ikigai doesn't have to be grand or life-changing—it could be found in the small joys of everyday life, like caring for loved ones, pursuing a hobby, or contributing to your community. The key is to explore what resonates deeply with you and remain open to your purpose's evolving nature.

2. What if nothing is at the intersection of my four circles?

It's normal to feel this way, especially when starting your journey. Begin by focusing on one or two circles, such as "what you love" or "what you're good at," and gradually explore how they might connect to "what the world needs" or "what you can be paid for." Sometimes, the connections become clearer as you take small steps and experiment with new activities or approaches.

3. How do I know if I've found my ikigai?

You'll likely feel a sense of alignment and fulfillment while living your ikigai. It's not about perfection or constant happiness but about feeling that your actions are meaningful and reflect your values. You might notice a greater sense of calm and motivation, even when challenges arise, and you enjoy the process as much as the outcome.

4. What if my family or people around me do not support my ikigai because they feel they know what's best for me?

This can be difficult, but remember that your ikigai is deeply personal—it's about what gives your life meaning, not about meeting others' expectations. Communicate openly with your loved ones, explaining why your ikigai is important. Balance their concerns with your needs, and try to make space for your purpose while respecting the relationships that matter to you.

5. I can't meditate. Do I have a chance to stop overthinking?

Absolutely. While meditation can be helpful, there are other ways to manage overthinking. Practices like journaling, mindful breathing, or focusing on single, immersive tasks (like cooking or gardening) can also help calm the mind. Find what works best for you and start small—ikigai is about adapting practices to suit your life, not forcing yourself into a rigid mold.

6. If I stop thinking, how will my problems be solved?

Stopping overthinking doesn't mean you stop solving problems; you stop obsessing over them unnecessarily. When you calm your mind, you create space for clarity and insight. Solutions emerge naturally when you step back and approach challenges with a fresh perspective rather than through constant mental chatter.

7. What if negative spirals keep pulling me back into overthinking and self-doubt?

It's natural to experience setbacks, but tools like mindfulness, grounding techniques, and focusing on your ikigai can help you regain control and prevent spirals from taking over. The key is to notice the patterns early and apply small, consistent actions to break free.

8. Should I throw away all my previous studies if they're totally different from what I like?

Not at all. Everything you've learned contributes to your identity and can be integrated into your ikigai. For example, skills from a past career complement your passion unexpectedly. Instead of discarding your previous experiences, look for creative ways to align them with your current values and goals.

9. How can I apply these concepts if I feel overwhelmed by my current responsibilities?

Start small. Focus on just one element of the 4-circle ikigai model, such as "what you love," and look for small ways to integrate it into your daily routine. Even tiny steps, like spending 10 minutes on a hobby you enjoy or practicing mindfulness during your commute, can make a big difference over time.

10. Is ikigai only about work or career?

No, ikigai is about your overall sense of purpose and fulfillment, including but not limited to your career. It could be rooted in relationships, hobbies, volunteer work, or anything else that brings meaning to your life.

11. Can overthinking ever be helpful?

Reflective thinking can help you evaluate options and make informed decisions in moderation. The key is to balance thoughtfulness with action. Overthinking becomes unhelpful when it prevents you from moving forward or creates unnecessary stress.

12. How long does it take to find ikigai?

There's no set timeline—it's a journey, not a destination. Some people may feel an immediate connection to their ikigai. In contrast, others discover it gradually via reflection, exploration, and trial and error. The process itself is valuable, so enjoy the journey.

Reflections on My Path

Looking back, I can see how much my life has changed since I began this journey. I used to feel like my mind was a constant storm of thoughts, pulling me in every direction. Today, my life has a framework—a sense of purpose that guides my decisions and helps me avoid the negative spirals that once consumed my thoughts. This clarity lets me move forward with intention, even when challenges arise. It's not that the challenges have disappeared. I still catch myself falling into overthinking, especially at significant crossroads. But now, I have tools to quiet my mind, refocus, and realign with my ikigai.

This change hasn't just impacted me—it's rippled into my relationships and work. Friends and family often comment on how grounded and present I seem. It's as if aligning with my purpose has created a sense of calm that others can feel. Professionally, I've stopped chasing every opportunity and instead focused on the projects that resonate with my values. The result? Greater fulfillment, less stress, and a deep sense of alignment.

I've learned that ikigai isn't about achieving a perfect life or checking off every goal. It's about walking a path that reflects your true self and appreciating every step along the way. I hope this book inspires you to discover your own ikigai and gives you the tools to live with purpose and presence. Remember, this is a journey—there will be challenges, but every step forward is progress. As you walk your own path, I'd love to hear about your experiences, triumphs, and reflections. Together, we can build a community that supports and uplifts one another as we strive to live with purpose and presence.

References

[1] Nolen-Hoeksema, Susan. "The Role of Rumination in Depression and Anxiety." *Journal of Abnormal Psychology* vol. 109, no. 3, 2000, pp. 504–511.

[2] Brown, Amanda. "The Importance of Social Bonds for Mental Health." *Psychology Today* 2023
www.psychologytoday.com/social-bonds.

[3] Pakenham, K. I., & Samios, C. "The Stress-Buffering Role of Mindfulness in the Relationship Between Perceived Stress and Psychological Adjustment" *Mindfulness*, 2017

https://link.springer.com/article/10.1007/s12671-016-0532-x

[4] Mori, K., Kaiho, Y., Tomata, Y., Narita, M., Tanji, F., Sugiyama, K., & Tsuji, I. "Predictors and Importance of Social Aspects in Ikigai among Older Women" *International Journal of Environmental Research and Public Health*, 2021

https://www.mdpi.com/1660-4601/18/16/8718

Bernadette Sakurai

Discover *Mindfulness Quotes And Coloring Patterns For Mothers*! – Your Personal Pathway to Mindful Motherhood!

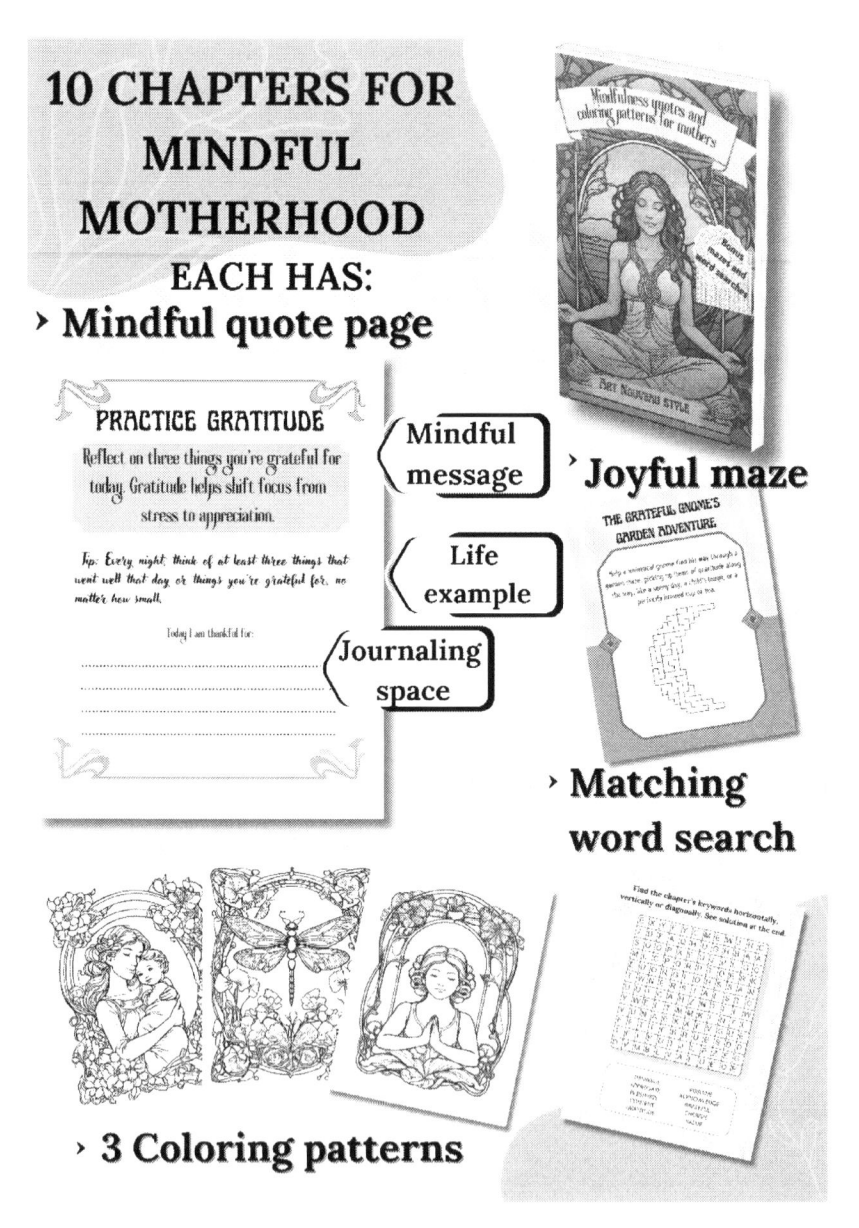

10 CHAPTERS FOR MINDFUL MOTHERHOOD
EACH HAS:
› **Mindful quote page**
- Mindful message
- Life example
- Journaling space

› **Joyful maze**

› **Matching word search**

› **3 Coloring patterns**

Printed in Great Britain
by Amazon

0b7b10d5-51b5-4332-9988-105259896773R01